Merging Mission and Unity

Donald Black

The Geneva Press
Philadelphia

© 1986 The Geneva Press

Book design by Gene Harris

First edition

Published by The Westminster Press®
Philadelphia, Pennsylvania

PRINTED IN THE UNITED STATES OF AMERICA

9 8 7 6 5 4 3 2 1

Library of Congress Cataloging-in-Publication Data

Black, Donald, 1920–
    Merging mission and unity.

    Bibliography: p.
    Includes index.
    1. United Presbyterian Church in the U.S.A.
Commission on Ecumenical Mission and Relations—
History. I. Title.
BX8937.B53 1986   285′.131   86-14847
ISBN 0-664-24047-X (pbk.)

Contents

Preface

Organizations are expressions of ideas. They are one means by which thought is translated into action. The Commission on Ecumenical Mission and Relations, as an organization, expressed an idea concerning a new dimension in mission and for fourteen years helped The United Presbyterian Church U.S.A. make a major shift in its approach to this work. The idea was that the church's activities in mission and unity belong together so that the one activity can affect the other. It grew out of thoughtful analysis of a changing world based in a faithful commitment to the mission of the church. This book is a reflection on the life of that organization.

In the 1950s change was required by movements in history. Nationalism in Asia and Africa was destroying the colonial empires that had provided the political framework for the missionary enterprise. International commercial systems flowed out of the West and laid the foundations for the transnational corporations of the 1960s and 1970s. An industrial civilization spread to all continents, reshaping rural societies and creating massive urban centers. People were on the move. Political and economic turmoil created massive refugee groups, and the migration of workers became a constant movement. Many Western nations saw their societies become a mixture of languages, nationalities, and religious faiths. Church people discovered that the former foreign mission concern for approaching Muslims or Hindus with the gospel was now a matter of neighborhood evangelism.

Change was required by progress in the missionary movement. Churches that had grown out of the foreign mission efforts were assuming more and more responsibility for the Christian witness in their nations. Programs and institutions formerly controlled by Mission organizations were being transferred to the control of the churches.

Change was required by developments in the ecumenical movement. Efforts toward unity had been led by individuals whose confidence in one another had surmounted confessional differences and had weathered the tensions of war between their countries. These individuals had successfully led their denominations into a commitment to seek ways of unifying their Christian witness and service, and ecumenical organizations were more solidly based in the churches.

Such rapid social change is exhilarating and frustrating, filled with excitement and uncertainty. It presents opportunities that become obsolete before they can be seized, forcing people to action without their full comprehension of where the first steps will lead. The decade and a half covered by the Commission on Ecumenical Mission and Relations were creative and ambiguous years, marked by conflicting and shifting movements—a time to live by faith. An understanding of the faith and a firm belief in the church enabled the Commission to move through those days.

The Commission recognized that it was an organization of the United Presbyterian Church and was bound by the confessional standards of that denomination. Within this framework it stated its understanding of the task assigned to it.

> The Commission on Ecumenical Mission and Relations is an agency of the United Presbyterian Church which, as a member of the One Holy Catholic Church, is empowered by the Holy Spirit to go into the world:
>> to make Jesus Christ known to all men as fellow man and divine Lord and Savior;
>> to enter into the common life of men, sharing their aspirations and sufferings, striving against inhumanity, and healing the enmities which separate them from God and from each other;
>> to encourage all men to become Christ's disciples and responsible members of His Church.
> In service of this purpose the Commission:
>> releases resources of the United Presbyterian Church for the mission of the Church ecumenical outside the United States of America;
>> explores and puts into action with other churches and ecumenical agencies wherever possible the forms our

unity in the Spirit should take in our ministries;
seeks on behalf of the United Presbyterian Church responsible participation in interchurch, confessional, and ecumenical organizations.[1]

W. Stanley Rycroft in *The Ecumenical Witness of The
United Presbyterian Church in the U.S.A.*[2] has given much
historical background. It is not my intention either to
repeat or to complete that work. It is my hope to show what
we thought we were about, to discern some of the forces
that shaped the Commission and some that impeded its
progress, and to trace the developments leading to its
merger into a new General Assembly agency structure in
the 1970s.

In some ways this story seems to be one of structural
reorganization. In the perspective of time it seems strange
that bringing together two boards of missions and three
committees involved with interchurch relations could assume such importance to the people involved. However,
we remarked earlier that organizations are expressions of
ideas, and the structures that had been developed through
history affected the attitudes of the church members who
supported them and of the staff who worked in them. "First
we shape our institutions, and then our institutions shape
us." These fourteen years were times when United Presbyterians were correcting some of the attitudes that had been
shaped by their history. What is now reported as the merging of organizations and the changing of structures is the
reflection of how new ideas were struggling to be born,
how people were attempting to express these ideas in new
organizations, and how churches were trying to develop
new relationships.

We are all products of our day, and with the amazing
clarity of hindsight it is easy to mark the mistakes of past
generations. Even though I was fully involved with the
committee that prepared the statement of purpose quoted
above, I am today startled that we could adopt such sexist
language in 1967! No one challenged such terminology. We
will find other examples where this organization, with its
liberal social attitude, failed to perceive important issues
clearly.

The terminology used in this book requires some expla-
nation.

The Commission on Ecumenical Mission and Relations

is often referred to by its commonly known acronym
COEMAR. It is also referred to as "the Commission."

The term "mission" refers to Christ's charge to his people that they should be his witnesses. Various scripture
passages support this mission.[3] When the word is capital-
ized it refers to the Mission organizations established by
missionaries in various countries—for example, the American Mission in Egypt, the American Presbyterian Mission
in Thailand.

The Board of Foreign Missions is often referred to as "the
Board" or as "the Foreign Board." Both shortened forms
were used by the United Presbyterian Church of North
America and the Presbyterian Church in the U.S.A.

"Unity" is used for the theological concept that all Christians are united by faith in Christ. They are part of the one
body of Christ; they are members of God's family. The
"ecumenical movement" is the attempt of churches to
express that unity through organizations such as the World
Council of Churches and the National Council of Churches.
I am aware that not all valid expressions of Christian unity
are included in this description of the ecumenical movement, that other cooperative organizations are almost in
competition with this stream of unity. However, for convenience in writing I have used the term "ecumenical movement" to refer to these cooperative organizations formed
by the churches.

I came to these experiences with COEMAR out of the
United Presbyterian Church of North America as that
denomination prepared for the union with the Presbyterian
Church in the United States of America which established
The United Presbyterian Church in the United States of
America. As Executive Secretary of the Board of Foreign
Missions I was involved in the discussions and negotiations
that prepared the new structure, and I was privileged to
serve on the Commission's staff for its entire existence.
Since this book is a personal reflection, the first person
plural is often used in describing group actions by the
organization.

During those fourteen years a large number of Commission members and staff colleagues contributed to COEMAR's
accomplishments. Not all of them will appear in these
pages, and I apologize to a number of competent persons
whose contributions are every bit as important as the work

of the ones mentioned. Even though a selection process is focused on events, it becomes unfair to some people.

Working on this project has renewed my appreciation for the more than a decade in an outstanding company of staff colleagues, Commission members, missionary friends, and church leaders from many parts of the world. Throughout this book I usually refer to them with the first name informality of daily contact. The events related here represent a portion of what they contributed to the mission of Christ's church.

A special word of appreciation for Ruth Reifel, who held the title of secretary in my office but carried the load of an executive assistant. Without her competence and efficiency many of the events mentioned in these pages would not have taken place.

My appreciation and love for my wife have grown as I review these years. One of the problems of certain career paths is the demand they make on personal relationships. Serving on the staff of a national agency of the church requires considerable travel, and the length of the absences from home increases when that travel is outside the United States. My wife accepted the demands of my work with love and support, often acted as a single parent, and regularly discovered the truth of Mrs. Murphy's law: "If it goes wrong, it will go wrong while he is out of town." Our children adjusted to the long absences of their father and have regularly stirred my parental pride. I am indebted to my entire family for making such a career possible.

1

Prelude

The missionary movement and the ecumenical movement originated in Europe and North America. Their histories were interwoven, and though there were different casts in each drama, each movement influenced the other in its development. The Holy Spirit stirred the churches in the eighteenth century in what has been called the pietist movement. A number of individuals across Europe felt God's call to carry the gospel to all people. The great expansion of the missionary movement coincided with the secular expansion of the colonial empires. The common worldview was that Europe and North America were the Christian parts of the world and that all other areas were populated by "the heathen." The white race carried responsibility for civilizing the rest of the world. It was against this psychological background that missionaries heard the call and Western churches accepted their obligation to carry on missionary work in Africa, Asia, and the islands of the Pacific.

The foreign missionary movement began as evangelism among "the heathen" who had never heard the gospel. The evangelists preached in the marketplace, distributed portions of the scriptures in the local dialects, and engaged in personal conversations at every opportunity. In addition, the missionaries' response to the human conditions they encountered led to other types of ministries, predominately teaching and healing. As these services developed, they were often seen as instruments for communicating the gospel message. In the schools, chapel services and Bible courses were required for all students. Evangelists preached in the wards and waiting rooms of the hospitals. In many countries the schools and hospitals were the main contact with society. In the background of all such effort was the goal of establishing a church that would become self-supporting, self-governing, and self-propagating.

The earliest missionaries ignored denominational considerations as they concentrated on communicating their message. The London Missionary Society, as early as 1795, resolved that it would send no Western form of church government to India, "but the glorious Gospel of the Blessed God to the Heathen." A missionary sermon in 1830 stated, "Nowhere on earth does the genuine spirit of Catholicism more prevail, than among missionaries, and the ardent friends of missions." A call to the Union Missionary Convention held in New York in 1854 said, "The approach of the time for a larger outpouring of the Holy Spirit will be certainly marked by a desire to seek for and magnify Christian unity."[1]

The sheer size of the missionary task required cooperation. To avoid competition, "comity agreements" recognized geographical responsibilities for the various mission groups. Missionaries helped one another in many informal ways and organized programs for the education of missionary children, scripture translation, literature production, and so forth. Regular conferences for missionaries from all denominations were held in India and China. Structures for cooperative work began to emerge. Mission councils in various countries provided a means for regular consultation and for working in the programs mentioned above. For example, the Foreign Missions Conference of North America was organized in 1893.

The missionary stream was not the only expression of a desire for unity. Confessional bodies that had similar theological beliefs and church structure gave a sense of family. The Baptist World Alliance was formed in 1905. The first of the Lambeth Conferences (Anglican) was held in 1867. The Alliance of Reformed Churches Throughout the World Holding the Presbyterian Order (often called the World Presbyterian Alliance) was organized in 1875. Its first General Council expressed the hope that the mission effort would not be transporting any of the various brands of Presbyterianism to other nations but would be founding a church related to the circumstances of the nation in which it would witness.

In spite of such hopes the missionaries felt that some church order was necessary for the guidance of their converts. They taught the new Christians what they themselves knew, their own style of church life. Therefore small transplants of all Western forms of church government began to flourish—presbyterian, congregational, episcopal. Denominational replicas were everywhere.

The tragedy of this development was that ecclesiastical divisions rooted in European history of the sixteenth and seventeenth centuries were transplanted into societies where such distinctions had no relevance. The Christian fellowship that new converts entered often became their new community, for many times they were expelled from family and other social relationships. But as they entered this new arena of personal security, they were indoctrinated into denominations whose limits had been formulated by theology and societal developments in another part of the world. However, they adjusted to this new framework for thought and worship, developing a certain investment in maintaining their new status quo. Fortunately the investment was not too great; and as these new churches became aware of the irrelevance of these distinctions, they pressured for more efforts toward unity. The movements for unity in the West have always been prodded by examples from other parts of the world. The Church of South India, the Kyodan in Japan, and the Church of Christ in China have been a psychological pressure on the churches in North America and Europe.

The World Missionary Conference at Edinburgh (1910) is considered the first milestone in the modern ecumenical movement.

> Three movements sprang out of the Edinburgh Conference. The first came into focus in the *International Missionary Council*, organized in 1921 to coordinate and assist missionary work throughout the world. The First World War had meanwhile made it clearer than ever before that Christians have a responsibility for social and political justice. This insight led to the movement for *Life and Work*. In 1925 this brought leaders from all over the world together in Stockholm in order to stimulate Christian action in society. The third movement, for *Faith and Order*, had its first world conference in 1927. This was to study matters which had been expressly excluded from the Edinburgh Conference, namely, the things which keep Christians apart and those which unite them in Christian fellowship.

In 1938 these last two movements associated to form a provisional committee of the *World Council of Churches* "in process of formation."[2]

The International Missionary Council was not a party to these discussions. It was composed of Mission councils or associations of Mission organizations, not of churches or denominations. In Europe and Britain the Mission Societies had grown up outside the churches, which were often either state churches or established churches. These Mission Societies had no direct relationship to the ecclesiastical structures, and they felt such contacts would stifle the missionary impulse.

However, in mission circles there had been a steady swing of thought toward the role of the church. The themes of the great mission conferences show this development. The Edinburgh Conference had been at a time of great Western optimism, and its organizers had been a part of the Student Volunteer Movement with its slogan: "The evangelization of the world in this generation!" The Jerusalem Conference (1928) placed Jesus Christ at the center of mission activity. The conference at Madras (1938) turned attention to the "younger churches" which were growing out of mission work. The Whitby Conference (1947) saw the older missions and the younger churches as "partners in obedience." In Accra (1957) the debate centered on the proposed merger of the International Missionary Council into the World Council of Churches.

The major point in the debate was the placing of mission activity into what was basically an ecclesiastical structure. John Coventry Smith of the Presbyterian Foreign Board staff raised the question of whether the mission of the church could be entrusted to the church. Even though it was a risk, he argued, the church is the instrument that God founded for witness and it should be trusted. This view won the day, and at New Delhi in 1961 the International Missionary Council became the Division of World Mission and Evangelism of the World Council of Churches.

The philosophy about mission that John Smith expressed in the Accra meeting had been followed by Mission boards in the United States for a number of years. In North America the "missionary societies" had become the official mission boards of the major denominations. The separation of church and state made this arrangement more acceptable, and this link to official church structure had influenced American missionary thinking. Mission boards anticipated a day when the responsibility and authority carried by the Mission organizations would be turned over to the churches in the mission fields. In the decade following World War II most Western mission agencies were attempting to give these younger churches greater responsibility for all the Christian activity in their area. In some Presbyterian situations such a step required the preliminary act of dissolving ecclesiastical links: the churches in Egypt, Sudan, Pakistan, Chile, and Cuba were overseas synods and presbyteries of the American denominations. Such churches could not be free and responsible for their own lives if they were finally subject to a General Assembly that always met in the United States. The Foreign Boards assumed that these overseas governing bodies were to be given autonomy, but not all of these bodies were eager to assume such a status. The Board of the United Presbyterian Church of North America had been raising this question with the Synod of the Nile for a number of years, but as a minority in Egyptian society the synod had found security in being a part of an American church. It resisted any move that implied abandonment. However, this process of dissolving the ecclesiastical ties with governing bodies outside the United States continued over a number of years—Cameroun and Spanish Guinea in 1957, Egypt and North Sudan in 1958, Pakistan in 1960, Chile in 1963, and Cuba in 1965.

These changes in the missionary movement began to affect the ecumenical movement, as autonomous churches sought membership in the ecumenical organizations. The national councils in Asia and Africa, which had started as councils of Missions and had joined the International Missionary Council, were now becoming councils of churches whose members were also members of the World Council of Churches. The World Council of Churches, which had been dominated by the North Americans and the Europeans, was having to adjust its style to accommodate to the presence of churches from Asia, Africa, and Latin America.

The Presbyterian Church in the U.S.A. had been dealing with the missionary movement and the ecumenical movement through separate organizations. Its Board of Foreign Missions was clearly responsible for relationships with churches that had grown up on the mission fields. Relations with other churches and the ecumenical organizations were the responsibility of the Permanent Commission on Interchurch Relations. Examples of this dichotomy occurred at meetings of the General Assembly. Fraternal delegates and representatives of ecumenical organizations were introduced by the Permanent Commission, but a church leader from Japan or India was presented by the Foreign Board, with the implication that here was one of the results of their work. It was not until as late as 1954 that the Moderator of the Presbyterian Church of Brazil was introduced to the General Assembly by the Permanent Commission instead of by the Foreign Board.

Following World War II another development came into the ecumenical movement—the growing concept of inter-church aid. Some steps for sending relief materials to churches in Europe had been taken through the provisional committee of the World Council, and churches in North America were looking for ways to help rebuild those churches. Inter-Church Aid became a division of the World Council of Churches. The program quickly expanded to help churches contribute relief assistance for any kind of disaster—floods, earthquakes, political upheaval. Then the program expanded to become a way in which churches could help one another at any point where there was a need. The Division of Inter-Church Aid, Refugees, and World Service was open to all churches that were a part of the ecumenical movement.

Churches in the West were then faced with two possible channels for assisting churches in former mission fields—the mission channels that had been used for years and the interchurch aid channels that were still in the process of being developed. Not only could resources be sent through these channels, the churches in the third world could send requests through either one or both. And since the people in North America who participated in the ecumenical organizations were not the same ones who directed the mission work, the possibilities of confusion, competition for resources, and so forth, were dismaying. Some adjustments by the churches in the United States were needed.

While these developments had been taking place on the world scene, the impulse to unity was pushing the churches in the United States to greater national expressions of unity. The history of the various movements in America had resulted in a compartmentalized approach to church work. Each mission board had its own department of missionary education and promotion, with materials developed separately from the educational materials of the board of education. Each board cultivated its own constituency. Missionaries on furlough would speak of having met some "mission-minded" church members, that is, people concerned for foreign missions. For years the boards were competing for the support of congregations and individuals. Unified promotion and a single general mission budget were post-World War II developments.

An illustration of the divergent policies can be seen in the strategies followed by the Board of National Missions and Board of Foreign Missions of the Presbyterian Church U.S.A. National Missions carried mission responsibility for Puerto Rico, Cuba, and the Caribbean. In the nineteenth century it was assumed that these areas would someday be a part of the United States. The strategy of the Board of National Missions was for churches in these areas to be fully integrated into the Presbyterian Church in the U.S.A. Ministers were enrolled in the Pension Fund, and the churches became presbyteries—Cuba in New Jersey Synod and Puerto Rico in New York Synod. The approach was a sincere attempt to express unity and equality across language, cultural, and national boundaries.

The strategy of the Board of Foreign Missions assumed that someday each church would be autonomous and shape its life to be an effective witness in its own nation. Salaries were related to living standards in the country, and the goal was for each church to support its ministry at a level proper for that culture and economy. The churches were being prepared for freedom and autonomy with a view to their taking an equal place among the churches of the world. Each mission board had reasons for its decisions, but it seems strange to have one denomination following such divergent mission policies. It could happen only in a compartmentalized structure.

This compartmentalized approach had affected ecumenical efforts. The Foreign Missions Conference of North America (1893) has already been mentioned. A similar organization provided cooperation for the home mission boards—the Home Missions Council of North America (1908). The International Council of Religious Education was the outgrowth of the first National Sunday School Convention (1832). The Missionary Education Movement of the United States and Canada (1902) was formed by the promotion departments of various mission boards, both home and foreign, and by boards of Christian education. The main ecumenical body was the Federal Council of Churches (1908), and its members were churches, not program agencies in a particular field. All of these various organizations, and some not mentioned, were drawn into one National Council of the Churches of Christ in the U.S.A. (1950). The new council continued the activities of all groups through four divisions—Foreign Missions, Home Missions, Christian Education, Christian Life and Work— and through a number of central and joint departments such as Evangelism, Stewardship, and Broadcasting and Film.[3]

Two streams run through these events following World War II. One was to bring into closer cooperation the various streams of church activity that had developed over decades. Another was to bring them into closer control of the churches as organizations. The early efforts toward unity had been through the vision and commitment of individuals. Often they were labeled "ecumaniacs" by those skeptics who did not share their vision. In the late 1940s and the 1950s the churches were officially strengthening the ecumenical structures and making them a greater part of their own understanding of how Christians work in the world. They were not attempting to make one church; they were trying to show that they already were one in Jesus Christ.

2

Preparation

The Commission on Ecumenical Mission and Relations was born during the preparations for the church union of 1958. This union was the occasion for the event, not the reason. The forces that were pushing toward merging mission and unity were evident in the Presbyterian Church in the United States of America, but they were scarcely felt in the United Presbyterian Church of North America. The latter denomination had established overseas synods in all its mission fields except Ethiopia, and that church was not developed enough to be involved in the ecumenical movement. The problem for the United Presbyterian Church of North America was to get overseas church organizations to accept autonomy. The Presbyterian Church U.S.A., on the other hand, was dealing with some churches of considerable sophistication, and the pressure in those situations involved participation in church mergers and membership in ecumenical organizations.

An effort to bring about a three-way union that would include the Presbyterian Church in the United States failed in 1955, but the Presbyterian Church in the United States of America and the United Presbyterian Church of North America decided to press on toward union. The time schedule called for a plan to be presented to the General Assemblies in 1956, voting in the presbyteries during the fall and winter, confirmation votes at the Assemblies in 1957, and the uniting General Assembly in Pittsburgh in 1958. That year would be the one hundredth anniversary of the United Presbyterian Church of North America, and it seemed appropriate for the new church to be launched in the city where that denomination had been formed a century before.

A number of informal contacts between the staff and members of the two Boards of Foreign Missions laid some groundwork for later formal negotiations. Staff members were often together in interdenominational committees. During meetings of the Division of Foreign Missions of the National Council of Churches the representatives of the two Presbyterian agencies would have a meeting. As the General Assembly of 1956 drew nearer, the staff contacts increased, and a recommendation was prepared for each Board to appoint members to a committee on merging the agencies. Such a committee would not be appropriate until the General Assemblies sent the Plan of Union to the presbyteries. Each Board appointed five of its elected members, including the president, and two staff members, and it began to meet following the General Assemblies of 1956.

Two things helped this committee in its work. The first was attitude. Even though the program and the budget of the Presbyterian board were five times as large as those of the United Presbyterian board, the committee representation was equal and the Presbyterian members acted as though they were dealing with equals. The second was a statement by the United Presbyterian president, Roy Grace, a pastor from Philadelphia, who was a leader in the conservative wing of the denomination and was known to be opposed to the union. In the early meetings of the committee it was evident that he was struggling with how he would vote when the matter came up in his presbytery. In the third committee meeting he confessed his struggle, stating that he would probably vote with his heart against the union. However, he felt that the union would pass and therefore urged the committee to make good preparations. This assurance that he would throw no blocks into the process gained much respect from the Presbyterian Church U.S.A. members, and the committee became a real team. Numerous studies and interstaff discussions were arranged, so that the process of putting the work together moved right along.

Joint staff and Board meetings were planned for the year following the confirmation vote in the Assemblies in 1957. Time could be saved if the two acted as though they were already one. A single agenda was prepared, the two presidents were in the chair, and each group was free to enter into the discussions of the other Board. For legal reasons the votes had to be taken and recorded separately, but the Board meetings were really combined activity. The first of these meetings was held at Pittsburgh-Xenia Seminary immediately following the United Presbyterian General Assembly. It was a mind-expanding experience for both groups. The combination of the work of these two denominations would give Presbyterians a greater involvement in Africa and would give the new denomination the largest mission involvement in the Muslim world of any Protestant church.

The joint staff work gave greater insight into the differences in style and size. The United Presbyterian staff consisted of four executives in Philadelphia, the part-time involvement of the Women's Board executive in Pittsburgh, and the Foreign Secretary in Asmara, Ethiopia. The Presbyterian staff had twenty-seven executives in New York, eight in area offices across the country, and ten field representatives across the world. It seemed natural that the smaller group in Philadelphia should do the traveling, so they spent much time on trains going to meetings in New York. The United Presbyterian staff were clearly the ones whose lives were disrupted by union. All of them had to assume new jobs and relocate their families.

Another shared activity was the furlough conference for missionaries and fraternal workers. The United Presbyterian Board held a "Pre-Conference" just prior to the New Wilmington Missionary Conference on the campus of Westminster College in Pennsylvania. A Board meeting was scheduled for the same time, and the Pre-Conference sessions became an opportunity to discuss major policy issues with the missionaries.

The Presbyterian Board held three "furlough conferences" in different parts of the country, arranged by the Interpretation Department and geared to helping the fraternal workers prepare for their interpretation activities. Some Board members would attend each one, and staff members were selected according to the agenda. During this preparation year a mixture of people from the two churches attended each of the conferences.

One other event took place in that preparatory year. The Presbyterian Board called its field representatives to the States for a full staff conference. The meeting was held just a few weeks prior to the uniting Assembly in order that the field representatives could be in the country for that event. The United Presbyterian Board invited its Foreign Secretary and a representative from the Mission in Pakistan. Discussions had already revealed that the administrative expectations from a field representative were greater than one person could provide for all the former United Presbyterian areas. The United Presbyterian Foreign Secretary had a different job description. India and Pakistan were the two countries where the mission fields of the two churches overlapped. When Pakistan was created, it contained a small section of the Presbyterian field and almost all of the United Presbyterian work. India had a small section of the United Presbyterian work with almost all of the Presbyterian activity. It was agreed that the Presbyterian field representative in India would add the United Presbyterian area to his responsibilities, and a United Presbyterian was selected for Pakistan.

The staff conference was held in Buck Hill Falls, Pennsylvania, and much of the time was given to discussing what the proposed new structure would mean. The field representative post was still fairly new, and there was considerable discussion of the effect of that position on the role of the Regional Secretary. It was evident that the processes and staff patterns of the larger denomination would be the operating pattern for the new church.

These efforts toward getting acquainted worked very well. The Commission on Ecumenical Mission and Relations was able to begin its activities following the uniting Assembly because the two major components had spent time getting acquainted with each other.

While these joint activities were going on with the mission boards, another discussion was taking place. Early in 1957, before the Assemblies had met, Charles Leber, the General Secretary of the Presbyterian Board, introduced the idea of the Commission on Ecumenical Mission and Relations to the Boards' joint committee. The plan was the result of discussions he had been having with the leaders of the Permanent Commission on Interchurch Relations. The plan was an attempt to solve some of the problems outlined in the preceding chapter.

The future of five organizations was involved in such a proposal. The two Boards of Foreign Missions were the largest and the only ones with full-time staff and with program budgets. The ecumenical relations activities in the Presbyterian Church were carried by the Permanent Commission on Interchurch Relations. In the United Presbyterian Church the Committee on Interchurch Relations handled union negotiations, while other ecumenical activities were coordinated in the Committee on Ecumenical Affairs. Each of these groups joined in recommending to the 1957 Assembly the establishment of the Commission on Ecumenical Mission and Relations. The details were to be developed and presented to the uniting General Assembly through the Special Committee on Consolidations.

At the Assemblies in 1957 each denomination appointed members to a Special Committee on Consolidations to prepare the new church structure. It was representative of all the elements of the two churches, and it invited staff members of the agencies to meet with it. Every effort was made to make this merger as simple and natural as possible. Subcommittees working on parts of the structure were composed of representatives of the agencies involved.

The Commission on Ecumenical Mission and Relations had sixty-six members, divided into classes of twenty-two. All members of the first three classes were drawn from the membership of the five previous organizations. Since administrative officers were confirmed by the General Assembly, the following staff positions were agreed upon and filled: Charles Leber, General Secretary; Margaret Shannon, Associate General Secretary for Ecumenical Relations; John Coventry Smith, Associate General Secretary for Ecumenical Mission; Donald Black, Associate General Secretary for Administration; Daniel Pattison, Treasurer. The first meeting of the Commission was planned for July, at which time it would elect its officers.

As General Assembly time approached, it became evident that among the enthusiasts for church union there was some opposition to the inclusion of that responsibility in the Commission. They felt their concern would be buried in the many responsibilities of the new organization. The disagreement was not settled through negotiation, though many efforts were made, and there was a floor fight at the Assembly. The church union group won, and a Committee on Church Union was established for "the purpose of church union and this purpose only."[1] It had twelve members, three of whom were named from the COEMAR membership. The early reports to the General Assembly reveal the frustration of a group whose church has just consummated one union and does not have another live prospect in sight. The normal ecumenical and interchurch contacts that might lead to union discussions had been assigned to the Commission. The committee reported its discussions with COEMAR about working relationships and understandings, but finally in 1963 (when those people who fought the original battle were no longer on the committee) a joint recommendation proposed that the Committee on Church Union be merged into the Commission.

Although the resistance of the church union group and the floor fight at the Assembly were a disappointment to many who had worked to bring the Commission into being, it did not dim the enthusiasm with which those involved approached the new church's pioneering effort at merging mission and unity.

3

In the Beginning

The uniting General Assembly of 1958 as its first act adopted a message entitled "In Unity—For Mission." It was a challenge to the congregations to be about the tasks of witnessing to the Light of God and mediating the Love of God. It set the tone for the new denomination and for the merger of mission and unity.

With great enthusiasm the Commission on Ecumenical Mission and Relations started out to be something different and to discover new ways of fulfilling the missionary task. Such a new approach is exceptionally difficult for a group of persons who have had their training and experience in a strong, older tradition. The demand to be responsible for an inheritance and the challenge to discover a new future create many tensions, and COEMAR experienced most of them.

The new structure was an attempt to deal with a future that was emerging on the horizon but that had not yet come to dominate the present. To be right ahead of time is to be considered wrong. Some of the problems that COEMAR faced were caused by its being ahead of its day.

INTERPRETATION

Early in 1958 the two Boards of Foreign Missions funded a special interpretation program to help the church understand the Commission on Ecumenical Mission and Relations. An appropriation of $80,000 was made to underwrite the effort. The special promotion called for descriptive literature, approximately one hundred regional seminars, special approaches in colleges, campus centers, and seminaries, and interpretative material or personnel as requested by General Assembly officers or agencies.

One of the most interesting items prepared was a poster. A number of artists submitted designs, most of which were in the usual traditional symbols. However, a symbolic hollow globe with a tree growing out of it caught Charles Leber's attention. It was related to the scripture passage, "The leaves of the tree were for the healing of the nations" (Rev. 22:2b). The poster broke most of the rules of communication. Its meaning and its relation to the Commission on Ecumenical Mission and Relations were so obscure that interpretative folders were sent with it, but it was used on literature during the special emphasis. There was no evaluation of this special emphasis. Once it was over, the task of interpreting the Commission became once again the responsibility of the Interpretation Department.

Two thirds of the membership of the new United Presbyterian Church in the United States of America lived within six hundred miles of Pittsburgh, Pennsylvania. The agencies agreed that a new area office should be opened in that city.

Area offices provided assistance in Women's Program for synodicals and presbyterials of the United Presbyterian Women. In this responsibility they each had a staff member supplied by each of the major agencies. In addition, COEMAR continued the Board of Foreign Missions practice of placing a male staff member for interpretation in each office. National Missions and Christian Education, however, supported staff in the synods who carried on judicatory programs. They had no need for additional interpretation staff in the areas. As the synods took on greater importance in raising the General Mission budget, COEMAR found it necessary to review the role of interpretation staff in the areas and eventually closed this part of its program. The area offices were devoted entirely to Women's Program.

The basic meaning of the name Commission on Ecumenical Mission and Relations never permeated the church, though there was an understanding of a new day in mission and support for many of the new approaches. The name itself was too long and complex. Many of us argued that it was descriptive of what we were about—seeing mission in an ecumenical perspective and relating mission to unity. Charlie Leber forbade the staff to use the acronym COEMAR in writing or speaking. However, before many months passed we reconciled ourselves to the fact that people were going to call us COEMAR and treat us as the Foreign Board with some added duties.

The distinction between a commission and a board was not clear, even in the minds of many persons directly involved in its work. The usual distinction in Presbyterian polity is between a committee, which makes recommendations to a governing body, and a commission, which acts on behalf of a governing body. Boards are neither. They are administrative organizations responsible for certain programs. In that respect the Commission on Ecumenical Mission and Relations functioned as a board and carried on programs in mission and unity. However, it was given the authority to represent the United Presbyterian Church in relation to other churches, and in that assignment it was a commission. In that task it was charged to use the resources of the entire church.

INVOLVING THE CHURCH

The approach of involving those resources in mission and relations was a break with an assumption held by boards in the past. Boards of foreign missions were assumed to have the competence within their board membership, staff, and missionary appointees to implement almost any program. Mission boards set policies, appointed personnel, managed investments, allocated funds, established programs, and interpreted their work. They needed no help from other agencies or governing bodies. The Commission on Ecumenical Mission and Relations, however, was expected to represent the whole church in mission as well as in relations, and it was charged to draw upon the knowledge and experience of the other General Assembly agencies in fulfilling its assigned task.

The new assumption on which this approach was built was that in the new day of mission the younger churches would seek help as they assumed responsibility for former Mission programs and as they prepared to live in the new industrial world. The Presbyterian Board had begun to develop such resources through functional services in literature, education, audiovisual services, and so forth. As COEMAR answered such requests from the younger churches, they were to call on the expertise represented by the other boards of the denomination. This assumption that the Western churches would be a source of expertise was short-lived. As events unfolded in the 1960s, it became clear that no church could claim expertise in mission, but in the halcyon days of the 1950s the church did not perceive such a change.

The COEMAR staff discussed with other agency staffs the ways of using their resources and even proposed the transfer of some former responsibilities to them. Two major problems appeared. In the Board of Christian Education and Board of National Missions there was no structure into which the concern for mission and relations outside the United States could fit. For example, the staff in the Board of Christian Education that related to campus work in the United States had no patterns of work that would relate to the problems being faced by the developing university centers in Beirut and Bangkok. The second problem arose because the staffs of these boards already carried full-time assignments. They could not take time for lengthy field trips to Asia or the Middle East and still do their jobs. Furthermore, COEMAR staff were not sure how much they were prepared to surrender. All of these programs involved church relations, which continued to be a COEMAR responsibility. After the early discussions, COEMAR moved cautiously in this approach, but some experiments were tried. Staff members from National Missions, Christian Education, and Theological Education were drawn into training programs and program discussions with related churches.

A method of involving other parts of the denomination in mission and relations was the result of another approach. In the development of the relations aspect of COEMAR's work the concern grew that ecumenical relations become the experience of the church membership and not be limited to a few official representatives to conferences and ecumenical organizations. Out of this concern to involve the laity in such experiences grew a number of involvement programs—seminars, "partnership in mission" youth projects, and laity abroad.

STRUCTURE

The structure of an organization reveals its understanding of its task, some of the political dynamics necessary for effective action, and the power forces that implement its programs. The Commission on Ecumenical Mission and

Relations structure was intended to show that both mission and relations were of equal importance in this new approach. It was also important to show the people from the relations stream that their interests were not going to be overwhelmed by the budget and staff that had been in the Boards of Foreign Missions.

The committee structure of the Commission was simple. The two major committees were Ecumenical Mission and Ecumenical Relations, and every member was assigned to one of them. Immediately we discovered the problem of helping the membership see the work whole when their committee handled only a part of it. We had established a Commission to put the two elements together, and then we appointed committees to separate them! We never solved the problem of communication between these two major committees. When we asked each committee to bring its recommendations to a plenary, half the group felt they were rehashing material they had already discussed; when we gave the committees authority to act and asked for only a report, half the group felt they had no involvement in what the other half was doing. Several systems were tried, but with no real success.

The other standing committees were Policy and Strategy (another name for the Executive Committee), Interpretation, and Finance. Special committees were appointed to deal with specific matters when they arose, and all such committees were reviewed once a year to determine whether they were still needed.

The staff was organized in similar fashion. The two main divisions were Ecumenical Mission and Ecumenical Relations, with an Associate General Secretary in charge of each. The General Secretary and the Associate General Secretary for Administration coordinated the work of the divisions and cared for general tasks affecting the Commission as a whole. The two departments of Interpretation and the Treasury were linked to the General Secretary and were to serve both divisions.

The Stated Clerk of the General Assembly conducts interchurch correspondence and thus has ecumenical responsibilities. He was therefore an ex-officio member of staff and was linked directly to the General Secretary and worked closely with the Division of Ecumenical Relations.

All executives were members of the Staff Council, and its monthly meeting was the place for drawing the various aspects of the work into a whole. All matters that were going to the Commission for decision had to be voted on by the Staff Council. The Administrative Council was the executive committee for the staff, and it considered policy matters along with general administrative coordination. Its recommendations were carried to the Staff Council for approval. Within the divisions there were subunits, and each group became an arena where proposals were discussed and prepared for their progress through divisions, Staff Council, Commission committees, and plenary. The process required endless typing of recommendations since at each step along the way there was the privilege of making changes, and this procedure was developed before the advent of photocopying!

This administrative style had been inherited from the Board of Foreign Missions. It could be described as "decision by committee and administration by minutes." Minutes became the record of a group's recommendations to the next level committee that must consider them. In theory all such recommendations had to be acted upon by the Commission. The result was that each Commission meeting had an accumulation of routine administrative items, known as "list actions," which the Commission considered in an omnibus action. Until some Commission action was taken on such matters the treasury would make no payments. Eventually we were able to get authorization from the Commission for the staff to handle many such matters, but that process required considerable change in the process of scanning minutes in each office.

This style of administration had some advantages. Any member of the Staff Council could question or make comment on recommendations that came from any part of the organization. There was plenty of communication and a sense of involvement in the total work. There was group discussion to help in reaching a decision, and a group decision to shield an individual executive from negative reactions. It was a method of participatory democracy long before the phrase became popular in secular circles. It also required a certain submerging of the ego. Major decisions and policy papers were so much the result of a group process that one could not identify the individual's contribution. One had to get psychological satisfaction from having been a part of the process.

The system had some disadvantages. Although it was an

association of equals, in any group some people became "more equal than others." Some staff members learned how to work the system, how to influence decisions; others felt the frustration of being outside the power stream, of not knowing what the dynamics of a particular meeting were. Such a system is appropriate where the work load permits adequate discussion, but crowded agendas give the impression that nothing is being cared for properly. On the whole, the system has more pluses than minuses, and it contributed much to the staff's sense of creative involvement in COEMAR's work.

Division of Ecumenical Mission

This division was organized along the same lines as the staff of the Board of Foreign Missions. John Coventry Smith, who had been Regional Secretary for East Asia and Associate General Secretary of that board, was chairperson of this division. There were three departments: Regional Administration, Functional Services, and Ecumenical Personnel.

Regional Administration

The Commission divided the world into five areas, with a Regional Secretary assigned to each: East Asia, South Asia, Middle East and Europe, Africa, and Latin America. The Africa office was the result of church union. The Presbyterian Church U.S.A. activity in Africa was limited to the Cameroun and Spanish Guinea, a single mission field. Responsibility for this work had been a part of the Middle East desk. However, the United Presbyterian Church of North America brought involvement in Egypt, an addition to the Middle East desk, and in Ethiopia and the Sudan, an enlargement of the Africa responsibilities. Thus the Middle East and Africa became separate offices.

The Regional Secretary was the main line of communication between the Commission and the churches and mission organizations in the area. All financial, program, policy, and personnel items were channeled through this office. This position had a long history in foreign mission administration. The pattern had developed that the executive was expected to transmit arguments the field advanced in support of its requests and also make a recommendation. This combination of information and judgment meant considerable power.

Regional Secretaries were expected to be the resident experts on their area. Through travel, reading, seminars, and meetings of ecumenical organizations they became familiar with religious faiths, political movements, and the overall mission picture. They became specialists in mission strategy, especially as it related to the development of the churches in their area and how those churches could be strengthened for their witness. They were called on for career and family counseling, often filling the role of pastor to the missionary personnel assigned to their region. They became involved in institutional development, especially in the light of how a particular medical or educational institution might fit in with overall mission strategy. At times it seemed that election to this post endowed a person with special gifts in a broad range of activities. In the perception of the churches in the mission area, the Regional Secretaries were powerful "bishops."

The Presbyterian Board had a large investment in hospitals and schools, and these institutions received a major portion of mission personnel and funds. This aspect of mission activity was so woven into the work of the Regional Secretaries that the Medical Officer and the Secretary for Education were members of the Regional Administration Department.

Under the former Boards of Foreign Missions the Regional Secretaries had concentrated most of their attention on the countries in which the Presbyterian Church had mission work. Their "regional" role was exercised when they participated as members of area committees in the Division of Foreign Missions of the National Council of Churches. It was through this structure that the Boards related to the various Christian Councils and to cooperative projects in their area. However, as staff members of the Commission on Ecumenical Mission and Relations when the number of church relations increased, they were given an opportunity to bring their regional perspective into denominational activities.

Functional Services

Functional secretaries were specialists in a particular activity such as education, medical services, literature, adult literacy, audiovisual programs, and youth work. The idea that a mission agency would have staff in such activities evolved after World War II when the churches were assuming increased responsibility for the witness in their countries. It was assumed that the churches would need assistance in developing these programs which had been introduced and managed by missionaries. Furthermore, the "knowledge explosion" burst upon society, and humanity accumulated an amazing store of new information about the world. This new knowledge brought rapid changes in these special fields, and practitioners were hard put to keep current with the new techniques available. It seemed important to provide a center where church leaders and mission personnel could secure information.

Several of the programs in functional services had a long history. For years the Board of Foreign Missions had a Medical Officer who divided his time between the health of missionaries and the concern for medical missions. Education had long been an activity of the missionary movement, but the staff Office of Education was not established until the mid-1950s. Cooperative programs in Christian literature, agricultural missions, and scripture translation and distribution had existed for years. However, the cooperative organizations in the West only served cooperative projects in the mission fields; they could not serve the various national churches. It was this specific church relationship that now concerned the Commission. When COEMAR was formed, there were twenty-eight national church bodies and mission areas with which the former Boards had been in mission relationships, and such a large group seemed to require the capacity to offer direct assistance. The functional services programs expanded.

Women's work has had a long history. In various denominations the women's missionary societies accepted responsibility for the mission outreach among women in the mission fields and developed boards to administer these programs. In the Presbyterian churches these boards had been merged with the regular Boards of Foreign Missions. Thus by the time the Commission was established, though there was still some involvement of the Women's Work staff in what happened abroad, the major focus of their activities was to provide study materials and staff services to the organization of United Presbyterian Women. However, Women's Work was a part of the Functional Services

Department and available to assist churches overseas that wished help in such activities.

Several of the functional services added an overseas dimension to what was originally an interpretation activity directed to the church in the United States. For instance, the Youth Secretary was originally assigned to interpret the foreign mission to the youth of the Presbyterian Church.[1] Literature secretaries provided study materials and audio-visual workers supplied films for the Interpretation Department. Since these individuals had developed competence in their fields, they were assigned to provide counsel when overseas churches asked for help. Their enthusiasm for these new overseas assignments helped stimulate such requests, and the functional services moved toward full-time assignments.

There was tension between regional administration and functional service before the Commission came into existence. The tension was built into the system, much like the "staff–line" tensions in the business world. In the secular administrative division, "line" carries administrative responsibility, and "staff" are the specialists who provide expertise. In this comparison the Regional Secretaries would be the "line" and the functional secretaries the "staff." If the functional secretaries had been content to offer advice on particular programs when asked, all might have been well. However, they assumed that they were in an association of equals and had some influence over the development of programs and budget in their specialty. When they tried to exercise their influence, they discovered they were interrupting a budgeting process and a flow of information that was centered in the Regional Secretary's office. Also, there was a sense in which the Regional Secretary was a "functional secretary" for church development. This staff person was the one concerned with how the church was developing its structure, concerned about what actions from the mission agency might help, or impede, its growth. All other programs were viewed in the light of these concerns. For years it had been assumed that mission strategy was developed out of the needs and opportunities in a particular country examined from the viewpoint of a developing church and its witness. A decision to increase the number of secondary schools touched on church concerns as well as educational ones, and the Regional Secretaries were involved. Annual budget requests for work in a particular country would include funds for evangelism grants, school subsidies, literature programs, and medical work, and they arrived on the Regional Secretaries' desks with no copies to the functional offices. Functional secretaries sometimes received information about budget and program decisions after these were well on their way to being implemented. The problem was rooted in a system that was well established and also insensitive to all the implications of a particular decision.

Some of the tension came from the way the functional services were introduced into the system. Charlie Leber, as General Secretary, at times used shock tactics to make his point. He stated that "functional service was the wave of the future." In providing these services the Commission would establish its new role when control had passed from the Mission organizations on the field. Regional Secretaries were told their days were numbered. At the staff conference in Buck Hill Falls in the spring of 1958 a paper was presented that proposed abolishing the office of Regional Secretary. It is a tribute to the quality and commitment of the staff that they did not blow up under the pressures. Later in the life of COEMAR we attempted to deal with such problems, but until then the staff had to work around them.

Ecumenical Personnel

The new day in mission required a fresh look at the role that personnel would play in the missionary task. Since the Presbyterians were doing away with Mission organizations on the field, it was assumed that missionaries would be working with the churches. The designation was changed to "fraternal worker" as a symbol of the changed relationship. This change was protested in several quarters. The term "missionary" had a long history and was loaded with many images. Some of them were good: sacrifice, a sense of special calling, commitment. Such symbols should not be surrendered easily. Furthermore, in some places the Missions still existed; no change in relations had taken place. It was finally agreed that where the Mission was still in existence the term "missionary" would be continued and where the church had assumed full control the term "fraternal worker" would be used. In the commissioning service that the Commission held for its appointees, people were commissioned as "missionaries of the Gospel of Jesus Christ and fraternal workers within his church."

It was assumed that in the new day of ecumenical mission the flow of personnel would be in several directions. In addition to those who continued to go from Western churches to Asia, Africa, and Latin America, people from the younger churches in former mission areas would also be called to mission service, and some would be sent to work with the churches in Europe and North America. All personnel would be a part of "the whole church taking the whole Gospel to the whole world." The Commission, therefore, had a Department of Ecumenical Personnel.

The Commission was founded in a time of expanding mission budgets, and the United Presbyterian Church expected to keep a large number of missionary and fraternal worker personnel around the world. At the uniting General Assembly in 1958 it was announced that eighty-five new appointments would be made, and in 1962 the number rose to one hundred and two. Support of missionary personnel was the largest item in the budget.

Efforts were made to recruit and train personnel who could appreciate the new dynamics of this changing world, who were quite willing to work under Asian or African administrators, and who could live through change. For years missionaries had been given special training in centers such as the Kennedy School of Missions at Hartford Seminary, but now the focus was on an orientation to the changes taking place in the world and in the missionary enterprise. The first experimental orientation program was on the campus of Hartford Seminary, but it was then decided that such a flexible program would have to be separated from academic structures and the pressures for degree credit.

A resort hotel in Mt. Freedom, New Jersey, was rented for the fall and winter months, and it became the first home of the Study Fellowship. Donald Smith, a missionary who served in the Philippines, became the director. The program was open to other denominations, and the United Presbyterians sent some of their new appointees to participate. The pilot program continued at Mt. Freedom for three years. It was a kosher hotel, and the participants had to accept the diet restrictions. It was interesting to observe how people committed to living in another culture found it difficult to adjust to a kosher diet.

The Board of Foreign Missions had been given a property in Stony Point, New York, about thirty miles from the New

York offices. In 1957 ground was broken there for the Ecumenical Training Center which would be a permanent home for the Study Fellowship. In addition, it was hoped that it would provide orientation to people from other countries coming to serve in the United States and orientation programs for people going abroad in business or government service. Don Smith developed a core staff and drew in other people for leadership in a flexible and creative curriculum.

The Study Fellowship program had many positive values. It was an immersion in the issues facing the church and mission. The appointees were exposed to leading personalities in the world church, received training in group dynamics and interpersonal relations, engaged in biblical and theological studies, discussed specific problems, and were then sent out to be in mission in a new day. They absorbed these five months through the filters of their personalities and prejudices. Reports from countries where they served varied. In some places they showed their preparation for culture shock, were aware of the changes they had to face, adjusted well, and were ready to learn even more than they had. In other cases new appointees arrived determined to avoid "those old-fashioned paternalistic missionaries" and prepared to be change agents who would save the mission of the church in a new day. The program reaffirmed the fact that ability to deal with change is more a characteristic of personality than it is of age, more related to security than to knowledge. Even though it was not effective with everyone, the orientation program was valuable in helping new personnel through a difficult period.

The Division of Ecumenical Relations

Margaret Shannon was the Associate General Secretary for Ecumenical Relations. Since none of the previous committees in this activity had staff, she was at first the only full-time staff member in the division. The original organization chart lists functions that the division was to perform—relationships with ecumenical organizations and with churches—and one department, the Department of the Laity.

In the early days there was much cross representation between the divisions. The Regional Secretaries were listed as members of the Division of Ecumenical Relations, and it was in this context that they would be required to move beyond their mission history and consider the ecumenical possibilities in their region. The Department of the Laity was at first composed of staff members who were also in the Department of Functional Services.

Ecumenical Relations became the means of breaking out of past molds and the limitations imposed by Mission comity agreements.[2] The Commission inherited a set of mission involvements in twenty-eight countries. In the minds of many people, both in the United States and abroad, those churches and those countries set the limits on how the United Presbyterian Church would be involved outside the United States. Margaret Shannon rightly insisted that, as a church involved in the ecumenical movement, we already had contacts throughout the world and were free to relate to any church anywhere. The ecumenical possibilities opened the opportunity for some new contacts without deserting the old ones. The responsibilities we inherited from the past weighed heavily, and the Commission took them seriously, but the concept of Ecumenical Relations kept them from overwhelming us.

Department of the Laity

The concept of lay relations shows how the Commission brought a new day for ecumenical relations as well as for mission. None of the former committees had this pattern in their activities. It symbolized the belief that ecumenical relations belongs to the people of the churches, not just to officials who take part in ecumenical organizations or to delegates who attend ecumenical assemblies. Programs were designed to put the people of the congregations in touch with people of other churches.

This development brought a new twist to some of the activities in the Department of Functional Services, especially to the work with women, men, youth, and students. The assigned staff members were a part of both departments, but in the Department of the Laity they were listed as Women's Relations, Men's Relations, Youth Relations, and Student World Relations. Here is an example of the shift in emphasis. The functional services concept was to offer assistance to a church that wanted to develop a youth program; the ecumenical relations approach was to put the youth of the two denominations in contact in order that they could learn from one another. It provided a new dimension on how churches together can go about their mission. Youth were not the objects of training programs to develop future leadership; they were being involved in the church and its work. Some of the Commission's most creative staff were involved in these programs: Kyoji Buma in Youth Relations, Margaret Flory in Student World Relations, Dorothy Wagner in Women's Relations, and Mateo Occena in Men's Relations.

Department of Ecumenical Organizations

As the Commission developed, the Division of Ecumenical Relations expanded. Staff were needed if the United Presbyterian Church was to participate responsibly in many studies that were being conducted by ecumenical organizations. There were some studies we needed to initiate ourselves, such as a restatement of our ecumenical position and a greater understanding of Orthodoxy. Staff were also assigned to coordinate our denomination's participation in ecumenical organizations. As some new short-term projects were developed with churches in other countries, staff were assigned to develop the programs.

The existence of the Division of Relations brought to the surface a problem about the status of the former field representatives.[3] Under the new organization their title was changed to Commission Representative, and in theory they were to represent both divisions. However, most of the duties they had accumulated were lodged under the Division of Mission. They carried considerable administrative responsibility, especially in communicating budget and personnel requests and in dealing with personnel problems. In a sense they were the overseas extension of the Regional Secretary. These duties drew them into close contact with the church that had grown out of mission history, and there was a question in the Division of Relations about their ability to break out of those inherited responsibilities and establish contact with other churches in their country. This problem was not a reflection on the individuals involved, but on the image the role of field representative had established in the minds of church leaders. Furthermore, they were assigned to one country. No pattern was established by which the Commission Representative in the Cameroun would be familiar with churches in Ghana or Nigeria.

One illustration of the problem comes from the Middle East. The churches that grew out of Presbyterian mission work are known as Evangelical churches, and even today they are seen by the Orthodox communions as a breakaway minority. The Commission Representatives, who had considerable administrative responsibility in working with Evangelical churches, would find it difficult to initiate new relations with Orthodox leaders. Yet those new relations were being established and were causing tension between the Commission and Evangelical leaders. At least this is how the problems were perceived in the Commission at the early stage of its life. The perception was not accurate, and the Commission Representatives in areas occupied by the Orthodox churches were able to make good contacts.

Part of the problem was the mood of the times. The spirit of nationalism was strong all over the world. Anything that evoked colonial images was suspect. The idea that a Western church would maintain its own representatives in other countries, or to cover a region, was unacceptable to many church leaders. They asked how we could talk of church-to-church relations when their correspondence was funneled through a Commission office in their country. This sort of pressure in the 1960s and 1970s would remove the office of Commission Representative from the scene.

The Commission on Ecumenical Mission and Relations was off and running. The early structure provided a way of blending two streams instead of letting one absorb the other. It also provided an arena where the one emphasis could influence the other. The process was not always smooth. A new emphasis often asserts its identity in negative terms: "We in relations will not make the mistakes that mission made." The old identity often responds with defensive attitudes: "We in mission must preserve the best of the past against irresponsibility disguised as dynamic creativity." In one such discussion I discovered I was defending not the Division of Ecumenical Mission but a caricature of it. I was defending a position in which I did not believe! Such tensions, however, forced a constant search for those actions which would be most helpful in the future life of the whole church of Jesus Christ.

4

Leadership
and the
Developing Organization

Organizations are people. The structures described in the preceding chapter provided the framework in which a number of creative individuals were free to explore an exciting future. It was the interplay of many personalities that made COEMAR the force it became in world church circles.

Over thirty executives and some seventy support staff worked in close fellowship. The missionary tradition was strong, for more than half the executives and several of the support staff had been in mission service. In addition, there were some from churches in other countries who brought an ecumenical perspective, some who were recruited from the American church scene, and some fraternal workers on furlough whose short time in the staff brought special insight into contemporary problems.

Charles Leber provided the impetus for launching the Commission on Ecumenical Mission and Relations. He had, in many ways, been the architect for "the new day" of the Presbyterian Church in mission, and through his ecumenical activities had done much to help other mission agencies in the United States adjust to change. Charlie, as he was generally known, was one of the last leaders in a generation that expected prominent and charismatic leadership in its church agencies. He was described as "a restless spirit, ever seeking more effectively to proclaim Christ as the rightful and only Lord of life."[1] Single-minded about his immediate concerns, he appeared aloof to many people; vigorous in pursuing particular goals, he appeared arrogant to those who dared disagree. Yet he was sensitive to people who needed his help, loyal in his friendships, firm in supporting his colleagues. The first three times he and I were in the same meeting we had to be introduced because he could not remember having met me! However, once we were working together, he was thoughtful and patient as I tried to learn the ropes.

Prior to the establishment of the Commission several persons in the Boards of Foreign Missions had helped to move the church forward. In every field there were some missionaries who were prodding their leaders to change. Among the staff, John Coventry Smith of the Regional Secretaries, Margaret Shannon in Women's Work, and Margaret Flory in the work among students were pressing for new methods. Glenn Reed, my predecessor, had been leading a policy review for the United Presbyterians. Evlyn Fulton, the first full-time staff for the United Presbyterian Women's Board, was a supporter of change.

Peter Emmons, a pastor from Scranton, was president of the Presbyterian Board and gave firm leadership in directing policy change. He was a close friend and supporter of Charlie Leber. Roy Grace, president of the United Presbyterian Board, was also helping to bring in a new day. Inez Moser, Katharine Parker, and Edith McBane were articulate in their arguments for new approaches. Theophilus Taylor, COEMAR's first chairperson, and Henry Pitney Van Dusen, president of Union Theological Seminary in New York, were strong advocates for the ecumenical approach.

The intellectual leadership was supplied by John Mackay, president of Princeton Theological Seminary and a true missionary statesman. As a missionary in Peru, as a staff member of the Board of Foreign Missions, and as the president of the International Missionary Council, he had been in the forefront of the missionary movement. He also led the church to a deeper understanding of the term "ecumenical."

Many people had used "ecumenical" as a synonym for "interdenominational." After the founding of the World Council of Churches there was a tendency to use it in place of "international." In 1951, when the World Council was only three years old, its Central Committee attempted to clarify the term.

> The word "ecumenical" is properly used to describe everything that relates to the whole task of the whole church to bring the Gospel to the whole world. It therefore covers equally the missionary movement and the movement toward unity, and must not be used to describe the latter in contra-

> distinction to the former. We believe that a real service will be rendered to true thinking on these subjects in the Churches if we so use this word that it covers both Unity and Mission in the context of the whole world.[2]

John Mackay insisted that some church activity was inter-denominational, and that there was activity which was international, but that the term "ecumenical" should be reserved for that activity which expressed the New Testament concept of the household of God as the witness to the whole inhabited earth. Therefore no one denomination could have an ecumenical mission, but it could participate in ecumenical mission when it consciously reflected its understanding that it was part of the "whole church taking the Gospel to the whole world." This use of the term "ecumenical mission" to replace the one-way direction of "foreign missions" was what the Presbyterians had in mind when they changed the Board's letterhead to read: "The Presbyterian Church in Ecumenical Mission." They saw themselves participating in a mission that belonged to the whole church. They would no longer speak of "our mission to Thailand" or any other country. The church in Thailand was as responsible before God for the mission as they were.

One attempt by the Presbyterian Board to interpret what this new day would mean was through a motion picture. Charlie Leber proposed a commercial film that would reflect the way the contemporary missionary movement was changing and the way in which the churches were trying to minister in this shifting scene. He believed that such a film released to the general public through commercial outlets would be a means of evangelism, that it would communicate God's concern for people in the midst of their human struggles. The Board agreed to finance the effort, and *The Mark of the Hawk* was under way.

The story was centered on African Christians involved in the independence struggles as new nations were being born. It showed the tensions among families and friends, the differences of approach among Christian leaders, the influence of the churches, and the help given by fraternal workers from several parts of the world. It was released just a few weeks prior to the uniting General Assembly, and its distribution and follow-up became the responsibility of the Commission.

The public response was not exceptional. The film's producer was not experienced in selecting distributors, the company chosen was in the midst of a management upheaval, and the release was during an economic recession. Many things worked against its success. At one point COEMAR wrote off a hundred-thousand-dollar deficit on the project, but television distribution continued for a number of years and much of that loss was recovered.

The major events between 1956 and 1959 were a drain on Charlie Leber's health. He felt great responsibility for *The Mark of the Hawk* and gave much energy to its production. The Lake Mohonk Consultation and its follow-up, the negotiations for starting the Commission, and the normal administrative duties were more than he should have undertaken. He was put under treatment for heart trouble during this period but seemed unable to let up on his heavy schedule.

The first year of the Commission's life was difficult for him and for staff colleagues who had known him as a dynamo of energy. His medication limited his participation in many meetings. He wanted to do his job well, and he was impatient with his lack of physical stamina. Though others on the staff were quite willing to share his load, and did, he knew he was only adding to their full-time responsibilities.

Although I had many contacts with Charlie as we prepared for church union, I worked only one year with him. It was a great learning experience. He expected hard work from his staff, kept the pressure on by advancing new ideas, and used argument as a way of stirring creative thought. He was an advocate for change but seemed most comfortable with familiar administrative procedures. That year was also a lesson in working with a charismatic personality. Colleagues were never sure how he would react, so they always had to be on their toes! They did know that his reactions were sometimes contradictions to one of his earlier positions. Such a style keeps people alert, and also proves frustrating. Fortunately, in Charlie's case the inspiration outweighed the frustration.

In August of 1959 the World Presbyterian Alliance was holding its assembly in Saõ Paulo, Brazil. Since this assembly was the first major church event after the Commission's organization, it seemed important for the General Secretary to attend. Charlie was known for his commitment to mission, he needed to show his commitment to ecumenical relations. Problems were also developing between the Commission and the Presbyterian Church of Brazil over Mission-church integration, and a special meeting with their leaders had been set for this time.

With considerable reluctance because of his physical condition, but under the pressure just described, Charlie made the trip. During the assembly he had a coronary attack and died. Although his death was a shock, it was not a great surprise. All of us felt we had lost a real leader and a great friend.

A number of Commission officers and staff, including Margaret Shannon, were in Brazil for the World Alliance meeting. Theophilus Taylor, chairperson of the Commission, consulted with the other members and made the following decisions: John Coventry Smith, who was on his way home from a World Council of Churches meeting in Greece, was asked to go to Brazil for the meeting with Presbyterian Church officers. I was named the Acting General Secretary.

Most people familiar with the Commission knew that if Charlie's successor was to be chosen from the staff, John Smith would be the selection. He had acted as Associate General Secretary in the Board of Foreign Missions in addition to his responsibilities as Regional Secretary for East Asia. The Commission wisely decided to make that choice without going through the long process of a search committee. John was elected at a Commission meeting in late September. I succeeded John as Associate General Secretary for Ecumenical Mission. The post of Associate General Secretary for Administration was abolished, an indication that it had existed for the political purpose of giving the Executive Secretary of the United Presbyterian Board of Foreign Missions some status at the time of union! Some of the responsibilities were included in a new post of Secretary for Administrative Services.

John Smith and Charlie Leber were about as opposite in personality as can be imagined. Charlie was intense and aggressive, John was calm and low key. They were close friends and had made a great team, complementing each other in personality and style. Charlie had once commented that his administrative principle had been to surround himself with associates who were as good or better at the work than he was. He had certainly followed that principle with John Smith's selection.

John quickly established his own approach to the work. He already had the confidence of the staff, and he was able to communicate that confidence to the church. He brought his own vision, showing a firm grasp of the issues before the church, a sensitivity to the feelings of people in a time of great tension, an openness to people of all persuasions, and a tenacity in achieving his goals. He was clearly the proper leader for the 1960s, and as the decade moved along he took on the role of elder statesman.

Margaret Shannon had many of the charismatic characteristics of Charlie Leber, and she could spin out new ideas faster than any organization could implement them. She was quick to discern new developments in the church and the society and was tireless in her efforts to get things done. She shaped the ecumenical relations part of the Commission. Her concept of lay relations and her insistence on the freedom of the United Presbyterian Church to be in relation with other parts of the body of Christ provided the breakthrough necessary for moving in new directions. She gave stimulating leadership to the Division of Ecumenical Relations until 1965, when she accepted the call to become the Director of Church Women United.

Dan Pattison, the Treasurer, had started with the Board of Foreign Missions as an office boy. He was the epitome of the American ideal of rising through the ranks. Fully committed to his work, he always helped the staff secure the resources necessary to bring reality to their visions.

The denomination's relief work was directed by an interagency committee under the General Council, but its funds were administered by the Commission. Through this responsibility Dan became involved with Church World Service and with the Division of Inter-Church Aid, Refugees, and World Service of the World Council of Churches. He became one of the important leaders in those circles.

The Commission was fortunate in the elected people who served as chairpersons. The first was Theophilus Mills Taylor, a professor at Pittsburgh-Xenia Theological Seminary and the first Moderator of The United Presbyterian Church in the U.S.A. He had been a member of the committee that prepared the Plan of Union and had served as chairperson of the Committee on Ecumenical Affairs in the United Presbyterian Church. In 1964 he used his sabbatical leave to serve as a consultant in theological education for COEMAR and conducted a thorough survey of all the seminaries outside the United States with which we were involved. He resigned from the Commission to accept the post of Secretary of the General Council in 1965.

Raymond Kearns, the second chairperson, was a pastor from Columbus, Ohio, who had been serving as chairperson of the Division of Ecumenical Relations. He moved into the broader responsibility with great ease. In 1966 he resigned to accept a position on the staff as Margaret Shannon's successor.

Charles Forman, professor at Yale Divinity School, was the next chairperson. He had been a missionary in India, had been active in student circles, and was well known to many of the staff. He continued until the end of his term as an elected member in 1971.

Dorothy Smith from Scranton, Pennsylvania, was the chairperson until COEMAR went out of existence at the end of 1972. She was the first Black and the first woman to head a major agency of the United Presbyterian Church.

All of these persons provided good leadership in directing the Commission. They were supportive of the staff and managed to create a spirit of teamwork in all activities. The other members of the Commission were active participants in its work, leading committees, attending conferences, and studying reports. Many of them served at considerable sacrifice to family activities and business responsibilities.

During the Commission's first year the Interchurch Center was being completed at 475 Riverside Drive in upper Manhattan. The Presbyterian mission boards owned the building at 156 Fifth Avenue, where a number of church agencies had their offices. That building was too small, and the National Council of Churches had offices in more than one building. Although the Presbyterians had agreed to sell their building and invest in the new center, not all of them were happy with the choice of location. Several of the staff had argued for locating near the United Nations. However, the Rockefeller family was interested in the renewal of Morningside Heights and offered to donate both property and money, so the Riverside Drive location was selected. We moved into the new building in the fall of 1959, two months after John Smith's election as General Secretary.

One of the pressures with which John had to deal was the need to examine our administrative processes as a staff. We were expanding and the work load was increasing. The tempo of life was also increasing, and our processes had been designed in a much slower day. Some of the laypeople on the Commission were involved in the new developments in the management field. They pressed us to get professional assistance from a new phenomenon, management consultants. None of our executives had professional training in the techniques of running a large organization. We were all products of on-the-job training by persons who were themselves products of the same process.

We selected the Hay Company as our consultants. Their approach was to help us clarify our decision-making processes. The consultant spent hours with us as we worked in small groups to agree on the accountabilities of each position. Hay Company argued that a job description is likely to tell people how to do their work; listing the things for which they are accountable leaves the "how" to their discretion. That statement is an oversimplification, but it was helpful in our case. It was a time-consuming process but provided some important clarifications.

It became evident that some executives had accountabilities that overlapped those of other positions. The most obvious case was that of the regional and the functional secretaries mentioned earlier. We refused to accept the line-staff relationship used in the business world, where one carries authority and the other offers expertise. We were an organization of equals and insisted that in such overlapping areas both executives were equally responsible and must agree on a course of action before any steps were taken. If they could not agree, there was a department chairperson to help them decide on a course of action. We worked out systems that showed how these accountabilities were interrelated and what sort of intrastaff communication was required. Much of the result could be described as codified common sense. We also reviewed what items needed official action by the Commission and what things could be settled by the staff members involved. In this way we removed much detail from our official meetings.

The process was not easy to keep going, especially as new persons who had not been through the review joined the staff. It required self-discipline and consideration for staff colleagues. Everyone had the accountability of checking with the other executives who might be involved. I commented that each staff member before taking an action should ask, "Whom should I contact in order to do my job?" A colleague came back with, "The question really should be, 'Whom should I contact in order that that person can do his or her job?' " He was expressing the ideal for a COEMAR staff member.

John Smith also instituted the Committee of the Whole. It was a technique for freeing the staff to discuss a matter without having to reach a decision. It became a time when we were free of our accountabilities. In these meetings I was Don Black and not an Associate General Secretary. All of us could take positions in the discussion that would be difficult to take if we were moving to a recommendation. We met as a Committee of the Whole to discuss policy issues when they were still in the formative stage and to give those preparing the policy position the benefit of our free discussion. Usually we found we were moving in a particular direction, and this preliminary discussion was helpful when we later came to taking formal action.

We also instituted Club 13 luncheons. In the building at 156 Fifth Avenue there had been a room on the thirteenth floor where the staff met occasionally for lunch to hear guests or reports from meetings and trips. We renewed the same practice, and these report luncheons in the Leber Room became a valuable means of keeping communication flowing in a busy staff and of maintaining a spirit of fellowship.

It is a tribute to the strong fellowship in the staff that many of these changes were effected with little tension. It is also a tribute to John Smith and his style. His concept of a General Secretary was of someone who made it possible for the other staff to do their work. We did not support him in his leadership role so much as he supported us in our responsibilities. The administrative task is to make it possible for something to happen someplace else—a church in Asia needs its schools improved, a recently opened area for mission needs a witness for the gospel. John clearly saw that the role of the Commission was to make those engaged in mission work more effective, and he epitomized that supportive attitude.

5

Early Emphases

The Commission on Ecumenical Mission and Relations built on the creative work of its predecessors. The Presbyterian Board of Foreign Missions had adjusted many of its activities to match its belief that the mission enterprise should reflect the ecumenical nature of the church. Although the denomination was not prepared to change the legal name of the Board, the letterhead read: "The Presbyterian Church in Ecumenical Mission." In Board meetings and conferences people from overseas churches participated. Four of the staff members were from other countries. The insights of Christians from other cultures and their perspectives on the American scene were considered a valuable contribution. A good foundation had also been laid in ecumenical relations. The responsible committees had kept the two Presbyterian denominations in the forefront of the ecumenical movement, and many persons had gained experience in cooperative programs.

The Division of Ecumenical Relations was just getting started, and it developed many of the new program emphases.

The Orthodox communions are a major branch of the Christian church, yet United Presbyterians had little in the way of ecumenical relations with them. In the Middle East we had much in the way of interchurch tension. The missionaries who went to that region in the mid-nineteenth century judged the church there to be virtually dead. From an evangelical perspective it was lost in incomprehensible ritual, in theological errors about the nature of Christ, in worship of the Virgin and veneration of the saints, and in an escapist spirituality which demonstrated no concern for evangelism among their Muslim neighbors. Although the missionaries hoped to bring a revival to this community, their strategy was to confront error head-on. The response of the Orthodox clergy was to excommunicate those people who associated with the missionaries and their teachings. The result was the organization of an Evangelical Church and a century of tension.

The Orthodox churches, however, were a part of the ecumenical movement. Several small denominations, which had been transported into the United States by immigrant communities, had become members of the National Council of Churches. Some Orthodox churches were a part of the World Council of Churches. Two observers at the Evanston Assembly in 1954 were the first priests of the Coptic Church of Egypt ever to set foot in the western hemisphere. They visited the United Presbyterian Board of Foreign Missions in Philadelphia and discussed the possibility of joint activity in the Sudan. They were quite concerned about the spread of Islam south of the Sahara Desert. One of them, Father Makary, remained at Princeton Seminary for a year of special study. He later was consecrated as Bishop Samuel, was responsible for the ecumenical relations of his church, and was a close friend of a number of people in COEMAR.[1]

The Division of Relations attempted to establish better relations with the Orthodox churches. One of the first projects was in response to a request from the Bishop of the Syrian Orthodox Church in Kerala, South India. This ancient church was open to new church contacts, and it was in an area of India where we had no mission history. Each year, COEMAR sent a pastor to them for a short-term preaching and Bible teaching mission. It was a good project for involving some pastors and congregations of our church, and it continued until problems in the diocese in India led to its cancellation.

This project revealed some of the problems the Division of Ecumenical Relations would have in initiating new approaches. The missionaries serving in India and some of the leaders of the churches related to our mission work questioned the right of the Commission to establish new relationships in India without asking their permission. They felt they had a right to comment on any use of resources in India by the United Presbyterian Church. If this project had been in an area of India where these churches were a part of the ecclesiastical scene, COEMAR would have consulted with them, but Kerala was in another part of the country.

It was one of the first occasions when the United Presbyterian Church had to remind another church that we intended to be free in establishing new contacts, and that we hoped they would feel free to do the same.

Another early contact was with the Orthodox Church in Ethiopia. The mission program of the United Presbyterian Church of North America had existed in tension with that church for some forty years. Government restrictions on the Mission and harassment of Evangelical Church members were attributed to Orthodox instigation. Official approaches to provide a new relationship had not been effective. A new channel of communication opened through the Office of Youth Relations. Kyoji Buma met a seminary student from Addis Ababa who was the Ethiopian delegate to the World Ecumenical Youth Assembly, and they set in motion plans for an interchurch youth caravan to Ethiopia.

The caravan was a success at opening contacts. The youth and their leaders were introduced to the head of the church, Abuna Theophilus, and to the chief priest of the emperor's church—Holy Trinity. Kyoji was asked to preach in the Orthodox Church at Dembi Dollo, the center of United Presbyterian mission work in the western area of the country. Later these youth secretaries helped further the contact by arranging a fellowship dinner for the United Presbyterian and the Ethiopian delegates during the World Council of Churches assembly in New Delhi.

This event was not without its tensions within the COEMAR family. The Mission in Ethiopia and the Commission Representative felt they had been bypassed in the planning and that they and the Evangelical Church were not given enough attention by the caravan. For a while it seemed that COEMAR was putting all its attention on this new relationship with the Orthodox and acting, as the Orthodox leaders did, as though the Evangelicals were a group who had broken off from the true church and would never amount to anything. The perception was erroneous; it was the result of having to share the attention for a period. After some time the Mission itself was drawn into a new relation with the Orthodox, and part of the reason was this early contact.

The Division of Relations invited some short-term consultants to assist in the study of Orthodox churches. Paul Verghese, an outstanding theologian and teacher from the Syrian Orthodox Church in India, served as consultant for a summer and then continued in close relation to the

Commission for a number of years. He had served as adviser in education to Emperor Haile Selassie of Ethiopia and gave us some valuable insights into that nation and its Orthodox Church. Paul Verghese went on to serve on the staff of the World Council of Churches, then returned to India, where he was ordained, consecrated a bishop, and later became Metropolitan Gregorius. He has been a leader in ecumenical circles for many years.

This emphasis on the Orthodox churches brought a change in our approach to the Middle East. Two women missionaries were able to work with Orthodox churches in Egypt. Norman Horner was appointed as a consultant in Orthodox and Roman Catholic relations in the Middle East. He conducted seminars, produced excellent research on those churches, taught courses in the Near East School of Theology, and established contacts among a number of leaders in the churches. His work laid the basis for continuing relations with this segment of the Christian church. As one sign of our interest in Orthodox churches we made a contribution to the construction of St. Mark's Cathedral in Cairo.

The Evangelical leaders were justifiably concerned that our enthusiasm for the new would warp our judgment. We might make some moves toward the Orthodox that would upset the delicate balance of community relationships. Egyptian friends argued that Bishop Samuel could improve things if he would be as open to the Evangelicals in Cairo as he was to the United Presbyterians in New York. They insisted that Bishop Samuel did not have much influence in the Coptic hierarchy and that we should be cautious in hoping for a shift in attitude by that group.

These discussions reached a tense point over the Coptic Evangelical Organization for Social Service (CEOSS). This village service program began as the Mission's adult literacy program. It would begin with adult literacy in a village, then add projects that would improve the agriculture, teach public health, distribute literature for the new literates, teach Bible courses, and establish family service programs. The program proved so successful that it was organized as a government-approved social service organization controlled by the Evangelical Church. As a showpiece of the church in social ministry it had expanded with European financing secured through the World Council of Churches.

The program served everyone in a village, and the Orthodox hierarchy expressed concern about Evangelicals teaching the Bible to their members. The CEOSS leaders insisted they heard no complaints in the villages, that this concern was only in the hierarchy. However, Bishop Samuel approached COEMAR with the request that the Coptic Church be permitted to have some members on the CEOSS board. We insisted that the decision was up to the Evangelical Church, but we finally agreed to raise the question with them on his behalf. This use of our "good offices" was resented by the Evangelical Church leaders and was perceived as exerting pressure. They felt we were being used as a part of Bishop Samuel's power play within his own church. It would be a feather in his cap if he could take over this very prominent and successful social service organization. They insisted it would be a takeover, that they had no history of being able to work cooperatively in projects with that church. The Evangelicals made it clear they were not interested in pursuing this discussion until there were signs of some change in attitude on the part of the Coptic Church.

The Roman Catholic Church presented COEMAR with another of its early emphases. Pope John XXIII called for the Second Vatican Council shortly after the Commission was formed, and Protestant groups were invited to send observers. The World Alliance of Reformed Churches selected the observers from the Reformed group, and COEMAR assisted with the expenses for the United Presbyterians.

The Second Vatican Council opened windows for the Roman Catholic Church. Protestants could see some of the inner workings of that communion, and the world was given glimpses of its inner struggle for a broader perspective. For a time the liberal Roman Catholics were in the ascendancy, and in many places ecumenical conversations about the possibility of joint work were taking place. These experiences were new for Protestants as well as for Catholics. After several months of what was almost an explosion of contacts and conversations, COEMAR took to the General Assembly in 1963 a set of Guidelines for Associations Between United Presbyterians and Roman Catholics.[2] The first session of the Vatican Council was over and some of the issues were becoming clearer.

This contact with the Roman Catholic Church continued through COEMAR's life. At one time there were conversations between a group of United Presbyterians and representatives of the United States Conference of Bishops. The United Presbyterian delegates were selected by COEMAR and included lay men and women as well as clergy. That selection turned out to be a witness to the Roman Catholics, for they expanded their delegation before the second meeting. Eventually these denominational discussions were expanded into confessional groups, and they continued their meetings for a number of years. During the 1960s there were many other contacts—meetings with the Conference of Roman Catholic Missions, consultations on Latin America, and joint publications with the Maryknoll Fathers. In various parts of the world Roman Catholic missionaries approached United Presbyterians about the possibility of joint work. It was a stimulating time which left its mark on both Protestants and Catholics.

The conservative evangelical wing of the churches was also approached for new relations. At that time these churches had not established any organizations within the mainline denominations, so it was necessary to contact certain churches that identified themselves as part of that group or some of the independent mission organizations. These officials were shy of contact with people who could be identified with ecumenical circles. Opposition to the ecumenical movement provided the raison d'être for some of the conservative groups, and they could not establish a rapport with the "enemy" very easily. One group of such mission leaders met with leaders of the Division of Overseas Ministries of the National Council of Churches, but everyone was invited as an individual and no publicity was given the gatherings. Such an approach established some personal friendships, but it could make no further progress until those individuals were permitted to transfer those personal contacts into institutional discussions. That step never happened.

The new contacts in ecumenical relations reached out to other parts of the Christian family. The Commission designated 1960 as Africa Emphasis Year and began a review of all contacts with that area. A special Moderator's Conference on Africa was convened and people from various parts of the church participated. It was during this conference that some of the liberal positions about society were attacked. One of the phrases common in political circles involved support for the people of former colonial areas in their "legitimate aspirations." The speakers at the conference asked, "Who determines what is legitimate? The colonial nations?" I realized that some of our attitudes in church circles had been along similar concepts of what constituted autonomy.

A Moderator's Deputation visited West Africa to carry greetings to churches and to open new contacts. Edler Hawkins, Vice-Moderator of the General Assembly, was the leader. His presence reflected the American black community's growing interest in Africa. It was a good visit and established new relationships. However, since it was a new approach, it had to contend with a mind-set developed in the missionary era, a mind-set that wanted to see what *we* could do for *them*. One member of the deputation reported how shocked he was to discover African pastors who owned few books. He was busy collecting books for one pastor he had befriended—the "missionary special" in an ecumenical era! Also, the churches that received the deputation felt they must show these affluent Americans their needs, so requests for help became a part of the visit. How difficult it is to move into the future when we carry so much of the past with us.

The Africa Emphasis Year was followed by efforts to establish projects in areas where we had not been involved. We also tried to use a different style than we had developed through our mission history. In Liberia we helped the church establish a school. In Nigeria we worked with the Christian Council in an urban experiment at Port Harcourt. We supported the Christian Institute in South Africa in its struggle against apartheid, and we exchanged visitors with some South African churches in order to discuss racial issues that were of concern to our churches. We provided staff assistance to the general secretary's office of the Presbyterian Church of East Africa and an organizing secretary for the first assembly of the All African Christian Conference, the predecessor of the All African Conference of Churches. We sent a gift to the Christian Council of Ghana, and they recognized it as the sign of a new relationship in which the donor exercised no control over the gift.

We also brought to the staff the part-time services of James Robinson, an outstanding black pastor in New York, who had founded Crossroads Africa. His program put students from American colleges into Africa on work projects during their summer vacations. It was intended to help

American youth know Africa, to establish friendships with the people, and to develop a broader perspective on world affairs. It was a very successful program and caught the imagination of many people in a time when America was accepting some responsibility for what happened in other parts of the world. Jim Robinson was designated as a Consultant on African Affairs. He not only gave good advice, he opened new contacts, and he helped solve delicate problems in relationships.

This new outreach into Africa was not without its mistakes. Since we were dealing directly with churches, we did not take the time to communicate with other churches and explain our plans. We established relations with the Presbyterian Church of East Africa, but we strained relations with the Church of Scotland whose missionaries had helped in the founding of that church. We did not even inform them of our intentions. We did not inform the Africa desks of the ecumenical organizations. We were not obligated to such contacts, and we would not want to give the impression to African churches that we were asking permission of former colonial masters. However, our failure to alert them only created the impression of a wealthy, arrogant American church buying its way into new areas.

This Africa emphasis showed the way in which the ecumenical relations aspect of our work could help us break out of the geographical confinement of history. In Africa we were no longer related only to churches in Cameroun, Spanish Guinea, Ethiopia, the Sudan, and Egypt. Once that principle was established, we were able to develop creative contacts with churches in several countries.

Another early impact on the Commission was the sermon preached by Eugene Carson Blake, Stated Clerk of the General Assembly, in Grace Cathedral (Episcopal) in San Francisco. He was invited by Bishop James Pike to be guest preacher during the assembly of the National Council of Churches. However, that assembly was not the platform for the proposal Gene made for a new initiative in church union, a proposal that Bishop Pike supported. In fact, Gene made a statement to the National Council assembly in which he apologized if his making the proposal had in any way detracted from their meeting. The Blake-Pike proposal called for four churches—Episcopal, Methodist, United Church of Christ, and United Presbyterian—to begin conversations about union, and it became the basis of the

Consultation on Church Union (cocu). The idea caught the imagination of the secular press, was given great publicity, and even raised hopes that a church union across confessional lines would take place within a decade. The staff work for the United Presbyterian delegation to cocu was handled by the Commission, and we were the channel through which their proposals were considered in the congregations.

In addition to these major emphases out of the Division of Relations, a number of program emphases were developing. Mateo Occena, a lay leader from the United Church of Christ in the Philippines, had originally joined the staff as Regional Secretary for Southeast Asia. He had been asked to accept a combined portfolio for Men's Work and Evangelism in the Department of Functional Services. He also carried the Men's Relations portfolio in the Department of the Laity. He proposed a program called Fil-American Teams of Witness, based on a similar program sponsored by the Methodists in Japan. The idea was that an American pastor and a Filipino pastor would work together in a parish in the Philippines, conducting preaching services, Bible studies, and other mission programs. Sometimes the Americans were with several parishes during their two-month stay. The program strengthened the congregations in the Philippines, developed some friendships, and helped a number of American congregations know something about the Philippine church. However, since the idea had originated in New York, even though by a Filipino church leader, it was criticized as a program imposed for the benefit of the American church.

Another aspect of lay work was the potential for Christian witness by people who were in international service for business or government. In the mid-1950s it was estimated that two million such Americans were living outside the United States. British churches had seen their laypeople as potential witnesses for several years and had developed special training courses for them. The Board of Foreign Missions had seen the possibilities and asked John Rosengrant to develop a program. John was a member of the Department of Interpretation to promote special gifts and had developed mission tours as a way of showing potential donors the needs in the world. He was somewhat acquainted with the problems and the possibilities. He arranged a number of conferences intended to attract laypersons who were assigned abroad, and the Commission published these lectures in a book, *Assignment Overseas.*[3]

These conferences were not successful in attracting people who were about to go overseas. We discovered that most pastors were not aware of such assignments for their members until the people were almost on the plane. Furthermore, once such an assignment is made, the days are filled with preparations to move, and the people have no time to attend a church-sponsored conference. Attention turned to approaching these church members after they were in their country of service.

D. T. Niles, an outstanding Asian church leader, was the secretary of the East Asia Christian Conference. He had had a long association with a number of COEMAR staff members and recognized our organization as one of the forward-looking groups in mission. In a discussion with Margaret Shannon he said that these American Christians in Asia should be a responsibility of the churches in Asia. Until then their church life had been in the overseas community churches that were a part of the "red, white, and blue ghetto" in which Americans lived abroad. If we would assign an American to the staff of the East Asia Christian Conference, that person could start to build bridges between the expatriates and the Asian churches. The Commission appointed Jack Collins, a pastor from New Jersey, who was stationed in Hong Kong and traveled the area with this responsibility. It was a new approach, and Jack worked with it for nine years before accepting a similar responsibility with the National Council of Churches. Jack worked with the community churches, and several conferences that related mission to economic issues established dialogue at a time when American economic power was growing. However, by the end of the 1960s the mood had changed. In the view of many churches, and especially in the view of students, Western economic power was considered demonic, and the Americans in military and business activities were seen as a major problem on the world scene. The multinational corporations were a force to be opposed, and their employees were perceived as a detriment to Christian witness.

The Department of the Laity was developing many other programs, all of them attempting to find ways by which laypeople could become an effective resource for the mission and unity of the church. Special youth caravans met and worked with youth in other parts of the world. Women's seminars studied some of the issues calling for the church's involvement in various regions. Students became involved in some of the new frontiers for witness. Many of the early efforts were experimental, but they laid the groundwork for a program that greatly expanded through the 1960s.

The Division of Ecumenical Mission was carrying on work that had been the responsibility of the Board of Foreign Missions. Its emphases rooted in one of the forward-looking actions of that Board, the World Consultation held at Lake Mohonk, New York, in 1956. Fifteen churches with which the Board was involved in its mission activity were asked to send representatives to the consultation. Months earlier they had been asked to provide information about programs, relationships, personnel and funds, and priorities. This consultation was an effort on the part of the Board to chart its future activity in the light of the best counsel from its related churches and with the participation of their representatives.

One of the most important results of this consultation was the sense of what the ecumenical concept could mean as these people from different cultural backgrounds came to know and appreciate one another. Cultural and national barriers melted, and a number of proposals about the future were made. Three major emphases became the working agenda for COEMAR's Division of Ecumenical Mission: integration of Mission organizations into the churches, leadership development, and "evangelism beyond the church." The consultation also revised the statement about the purpose of the Christian mission. An earlier statement had reflected the one-way perspective of the foreign mission era; the new statement could express the concerns of the church anywhere in the world. Its revised form has already been quoted in the Preface.

In every country to which the Boards of Foreign Missions had sent mission personnel a Mission had been established. In the United Presbyterian Church of North America mission fields it was called The American Mission, and in Presbyterian areas it was known as The American Presbyterian Mission. Quite often these organizations had legal status in the countries in order to hold property, represent the missionaries before the government, enter into contracts for running schools, import materials from abroad, and so forth. Membership was usually composed of the missionaries who had been appointed by the Board. It was a democratic organization, with each member having a vote. Since missionary wives were appointed along with their husbands, they had a vote and participated fully in the work of the mission—a partial liberation of women!

The Mission was responsible for all the programs and institutions in its area. It developed strategy for evangelistic outreach, determined the location of schools and hospitals, supervised the orientation and language study of new missionaries, set salaries for native evangelists, entered into negotiations with government administrators about educational and health services, and developed the machinery necessary for a group of expatriates to operate in a different culture.

The Mission structure and its institutions had been developed along Western ideas. There was not much choice in this matter. Educational, medical, and social services were controlled by colonial governments. School systems were usually a transplant from the home country. The American Universities in Cairo and Beirut were attempts to introduce the American educational system into a British and a French system, and though they were permitted to operate, their degrees had no official standing in the national educational system. In some cases the Missions agreed to run schools for the government; in other cases the Missions ran private schools, but always they had to operate within government standards. These standards were set by Westerners who were bringing "the blessings of civilization" to these nations. The same pattern applied to other social service activities. The assumption of the time was that it was the responsibility of the Western nations to civilize the rest of the world. Since Western civilization was considered the product of the gospel's influence on human society, it was a legitimate activity for Missions to join.

"The Mission" had become a very powerful organization in relation to the church in its area. The schools represented the key to a secure future for Christian children and provided jobs for many church members. The persons who controlled school admissions and the persons who hired teachers were powerful people. The hospitals represented jobs, health, and even life for many people who could not afford to pay for medical services. Control of hospital fees was another powerful influence. The evangelism program represented livelihood for all local evangelists and many pastors. When a congregation was located near a large mission school or hospital, the institutional jobs represented the financial support of the congregation. The Mission was also the door to the church in the United States, the source of the money that paid the salaries and supported the institutions. Some resources were secured through school fees and government grants, but church leaders were not brought into the management side of the Mission enough to know the various sources of program support.

The Missions had operated this power structure for over a century, and they had trusted two principles: the Christian commitment of the missionaries and the checks and balances of committee administration.

The assumption was that everyone in the Mission was basically honest, but some missionaries did use bad judgment in dispensing funds, some overspent their salaries and had to be helped out of debt, and some were not trained for business activities. The auditing procedures were to catch mistakes rather than prevent theft.

The other principle was administration by committee. Where two or three missionaries were located in one place, there had to be a station meeting. Matters such as housing arrangements, schedules for the use of cars, approval of house repairs, and new program ideas were hashed out in station meetings. The Mission had committees to propose general rules, to supervise overall strategy, and to coordinate the work of the stations. The Mission met once a year to review work and make plans for the future. It was a combination of old home week, business, worship, fellowship, and inspiration.

The existence of such a Western-style organization was not of major concern to most people. They worked on the assumption that the developing church would progressively assume responsibility for the Mission programs. The church supported its pastors and controlled its ecclesiastical affairs. In many cases the churches took over the village elementary schools and small clinics. Eventually the work would all be transferred to the churches, the Mission would be disbanded, and all missionaries would have "worked themselves out of their jobs" and would go home. The term used in mission circles for this process was "devolution."

Time was not on the side of such a deliberate approach. The spirit of independence pervading the new nations and the younger churches would not tolerate an organization that held so much power over the lives and the future of so many church people. The strategy proposed out of Lake Mohonk was to integrate the Mission programs into the life of the churches with the understanding that the church in the United States would continue to assist in their support and former missionaries would assist in their operation. We would be "partners in obedience."

Once the principle of integration was adopted by the Board of Foreign Missions it was up to the church leaders and the representatives of the Mission and the Board to work out the local process. Although we used the phrase "integration of Mission and church," it was necessary for the church to develop its own structures to manage the Mission programs. It was not assumed that the Mission as an organization would just be loaded on the church, for the latter might be overwhelmed. Church governing bodies might become the arena for power plays over the control of institutions. We were not successful in avoiding this danger, and in some areas the churches did become preoccupied with running institutions and programs, and everyone suffered.

Another problem was the double use of the word "mission." We speak of "the mission of the church" when we think of the charge Christ gave his people. We say that a denomination feels a mission responsibility for Egypt when it decides to send missionaries to that country. This use of the term is a part of the church's *theological* vocabulary. The missionaries in Egypt form an organization known as the Mission, and the word has become a part of the church's *administrative* vocabulary. We were not always clear about which vocabulary we were using, and confusion was the result. The following example shows the shift in strategy that took place at the Mohonk Consultation and one of the problems that resulted.

For a century the Presbyterian Church had claimed that it had a mission from God to communicate the gospel to the people of Syria and Lebanon—a part of our theological understanding. In order to be faithful to that mission we organized a Mission in Syria and Lebanon to conduct various programs: evangelism, schools, hospitals, and others—a part of our church's administrative structure. We expected that a church would result from this activity, that it would be called by God to carry out the mission (theo-

logical concept) in Syria and Lebanon, and as it accepted
that responsibility, the programs and institutions being run
by the Presbyterian Church through its Mission (administrative) would be transferred to this church, the Mission
would be dissolved, and the Presbyterians in the United
States would feel that their mission (theological) in those
countries had been completed. In this way, "devolution"
dominated Presbyterian missionary thinking until the
Mohonk Consultation.

A theological shift had taken place in ecumenical mission circles following World War II. Missionary strategists
were describing the Western mission agencies and the new
churches in the mission fields as "partners in obedience."[4]
They no longer saw a time when the Western churches
would be relieved of their mission (theological) responsibility and could "go home" with a feeling of a job well
done. Nor could the younger churches wait until some
time when they were able to assume full direction and
support of the Mission programs (administrative) to hear
God's call to mission (theological), the responsibility of
mission was placed on all believers when they became a
part of the church. The whole church must take the whole
gospel to the whole world.

The Presbyterian Board of Foreign Missions was searching for ways to express this new understanding that the
missionary task was shared by all churches. At Mohonk
the policy decision was to integrate the Missions into the
churches in the various countries. In Syria-Lebanon,
therefore, the American Presbyterian Mission was to be
integrated into the Synod of the Evangelical Church. The
synod was to be responsible for the mission (theological
concept) in those countries, and the Presbyterian Church
would work with it as a partner. "The mission belongs to
the church" was the theological concept we were expressing, but the process meant that the church heard an
administrative concept: "The Mission belongs to the
church." Since the Mission had been the administrative
arm of the Presbyterian Church, the partner churches
now assumed they were the administrative arm of the
Presbyterian Church in the United States of America.
Instead of giving a feeling of independence to those
church leaders, we were in process of making them feel
that they were the branch office of a worldwide ecclesi-

astical corporation whose head offices were in New York. Correcting this impression took much time and created new tensions.

One of the saving approaches in dealing with this problem came through the ecumenical relations emphasis. When we began to relate to other churches we were asserting our autonomy as a church involved in both ecumenical mission and relations. We had no branches overseas! The mission (theological) of the church belonged to the whole church, and our mission and relations activities were to be a part of the whole church taking the whole gospel to the whole world.

Another emphasis from the Mohonk Consultation was leadership development. The Board of Foreign Missions had maintained a scholarship program for a number of years. As the churches were assuming more responsibility for programs and institutions, it was important that people be trained in the techniques of directing these sophisticated Western-style organizations. Some institutions in other nations were developing the capacity to offer such training, and the consultation proposed greater use of those institutions.

The leadership development emphasis had been a part of the Student Work office. Some excellent programs were implemented, and many of the leaders in churches and ecumenical organizations were participants. A separate Office of Leadership Development was set up and the whole approach reviewed. Early scholarship programs operated on limited funds, so grants were usually limited to one year. Budget considerations precluded bringing families, and long separations resulted in family problems.

The Leadership Development Office developed processes by which the churches selected the persons for whom they wished training and the particular jobs for which the persons were to be prepared, and they assured them that the job would be theirs when studies were completed. If the training required more than a year, plans were made to fund the course and to bring the family with the student. A survey after ten years revealed that one third of those in our program were being trained outside the United States, and 90 percent of those who had been trained were at the tasks for which they had been selected.

A third emphasis at Lake Mohonk was "evangelism beyond the church," an effort to reach the community beyond those people who would normally be touched by preaching and worship services.

Drama and the arts were seen as instruments in this effort. One of the first efforts was some consultations with artists and dramatists, and one of the themes was "Drama as an Instrument of Evangelism." The dramatists quickly made it clear that their professions were not tools to be used by the churches. Drama and the arts have integrity in themselves. The artists are expressing truth as they perceive it. If that person is a Christian, then that perception will be informed by the faith, but neither drama nor the arts should be treated as instruments of communication. We changed our approach and concentrated on the relationship between the arts and the gospel. In a short time we established the Office of Fine Arts which worked with churches on how indigenous art forms could be related to the gospel. A number of Christian artists were supported in their efforts to express their faith in their art.

A barn on the property at Stony Point was remodeled into a small theater, and for a number of years the Commission sponsored the Barn Playhouse each summer. An international company of students, missionaries, and church leaders engaged in study and in dramas that came from all parts of the world and had themes related to the gospel. It was a good experience and some fine work was done. However, the Commission could not fully subsidize it, and the income from the plays was an important part of the budget. The tension between the training activities and the pressure to produce income was an important factor in the closing of the program.

The Mass Media program was a major part of "evangelism beyond the church." New techniques were available as technology improved. Major broadcasting centers had been established in Korea, the Philippines, and Ethiopia. The last two were shortwave with a range over the whole region. In almost every major city there was a studio producing materials in local language to be sent to the main center for broadcast. The cost of setting up and maintaining such installations required funding from a number of sources. The Commission staff played a leading role in the international cooperative efforts to support such projects. In addition, the development of audiovisual materials and equipment and the training of church workers in their use became an important program.

Literacy and Literature programs expanded. Several years before this time a new technique for teaching adults to read was developed by Frank Laubach, a missionary in the Philippines. This method of "each one teach one" spread through the mission fields, and adulv literacy programs became an important activity. The new literates needed reading material scaled to their abilities, so training programs for writers were started. Christian publishing activities expanded.

Special activities in education also developed. The Office of Education devised a technique for helping churches upgrade their educational work. A team of educators from several countries, many of whom faced problems similar to those in the church they were to visit, would spend several weeks with a church, surveying its schools, examining the relation to public education, and meeting with church leaders, school administrators, teachers, and government officials. They worked out ways by which the church could increase the effectiveness of its educational ministries. The survey reports became the working document for several months of follow-up activity.

One of the early emphases in the Division of Ecumenical Mission came out of the United Presbyterian Church of North America. In 1956 its Board of Foreign Missions was struggling with the problem of teaching Islam in the Mission schools in Egypt. The pressure by the Egyptian government to permit such teaching was one of the signs of a resurgent Islam. Glenn Reed, Foreign Secretary, suggested a study conference on mission in the Muslim world. Islam seemed to be spreading into Africa south of the Sahara and was considered a threat to the Christian mission effort. Indonesia would be a new Muslim state in the Pacific, and Pakistan had been created for the Muslim population of the Indian subcontinent.

The staff in Philadelphia responded to Glenn's idea with enthusiasm. Negotiations for union were far enough along to suggest clearance with the Presbyterian Board before going ahead, and they appropriated some funds toward it. The planning committee involved several field representatives and staff members from both Boards. During the planning for the conference it became clear that the new United Presbyterian Church U.S.A. would have the most extensive mission involvement in the Muslim world of any Protestant denomination, extending from the Sudan in Africa to Indonesia in the Pacific.

The name of the conference was Christian Faith and the Contemporary Middle Eastern World. The name avoided any direct reference to Islam so that Muslim governments would not refuse exit visas to participants. Though it was called by the United Presbyterian Church, invitations were sent to a large number of churches, missions, and ecumenical organizations. There was a very good response, and many who attended appreciated the fresh look at the missionary task in the light of changes that both Christians and Muslims were experiencing in the modern world. Kenneth Cragg, an Anglican scholar, was reviving Christian interest in understanding Islam, and many Muslim scholars were trying to achieve some accommodation between the Koran and modern scientific knowledge.

The approach of the conference was to see whether Christians could cooperate with Muslims on matters of common human concern instead of confronting them on matters of theology. Through such cooperation, dialogue might be established on matters of faith and the opportunity for witness would arise. The historic barriers between the two faiths had blocked communication, and we were searching for a new approach.

Two decades later it seems strange that a conference such as this one did not perceive the strength of the conservative forces in Islam, forces epitomized by the revolution in Iran. Mission leaders knew of efforts to strengthen Islam, but they saw the conservative efforts as political moves against particular liberal leaders. Conservative trends were perceived as aberrations in a changing world, aberrations that the Muslim society itself would handle.

Three specific recommendations were made. One was an increased use of broadcasting, and COEMAR gave good support to the radio station in Addis Ababa as well as supporting the local studios which prepared materials. The second was to use more non-American mission personnel in the area, but this effort had limited success. The third, a joint mission effort with some of the churches, never got under way. This conference was helpful to those who attended, but in the long run it had little effect on the churches or on the mission effort in the Muslim world.

The program of Fraternal Workers to the U.S.A. had

started under the Presbyterian Board and was continued under the Commission. This program placed people from churches in other countries into United Presbyterian congregations and governing bodies for special assignments. The first participants were from Europe and were able to fit into some urban programs and other activities. As the invitations went out to other countries, the programs became more difficult to develop. The new fraternal workers needed help in adjusting to life in America, and local church members did not always know how to be helpful. Most Americans had little experience in trying to relate across cultural barriers. Although the intentions were always the best, the experience was not always a good one.

We discovered that many American Christians were not prepared to learn from someone of a different culture, nor did they have the patience to listen through difficult accents. Few people in the pews were aware that they were being subjected to the same experience that their missionaries had inflicted upon people in other parts of the world, for not all missionaries became experts in the language they were expected to use. These problems only emphasized the need for the church in the United States to see its own society as an object of God's mission to all people.

There was some concern in the missionary community when this program was initiated, especially when some overseas church leaders were called to service on the staff in New York. Some of the most able persons were called from churches already thin in leadership. Extended service in the West might alienate people from their culture, and the missionaries were concerned about the capacity of the younger churches to provide jobs that would challenge people with such experience to return. These concerns were held by the staff as well, but the total mission could not go forward unless all churches were willing to face all of its costs.

Property transfers became an important part of COEMAR's work. Much work was needed to clear titles, for property had been obtained in many different ways through the years. Sometimes a missionary bought property for a mission station and had it registered in his name because that was the only legal option. Sometimes property was donated by a friendly government and put in the name of the Mission. Some property titles were in the name of the Board of Foreign Missions or one of its predecessor organizations. As governments changed or mission offices shifted, the files were not always protected. In some countries COEMAR had people working full time at property matters.

With the policy decision to transfer power from the Missions into the churches, transferring property to the churches became an important activity. In some countries the tax on transferring property almost equaled the selling price, and donating the property did not escape the tax. No one could afford to pay such large sums, and years went by as legal and government experts were consulted in an effort to find a way around such expense.

Many of the churches did not have legal entities that could hold property. It took time to decide what sort of legal body they wanted to hold and manage their property, and getting such an organization registered was an additional expense.

The transfer of property was a mixed blessing to the churches. The Commission had self-insured the property it owned, but the church had to purchase such protection. Maintenance of the buildings became a problem to the churches and institutions, for the Commission was not able to provide all the funds required.

Some of the property that COEMAR owned was not being used. It had been secured at a time when there were plans for expansion of work, but later decisions changed the plans. Such property often had good value in the secular market, but it was difficult to get the church people to agree to sell. As minority communities, they were reluctant to sell any property. In Pakistan the church argued that it would have great difficulty getting permission to buy any more property, and it wanted us to sell none of what we held.

When property that had been bought for mission program was sold, the proceeds were used in that country. These funds were used to pay expenses related to the transfer of other property, but those expenses seldom exhausted the money received. Sometimes the receipts were used to help the church start a pension fund or to meet other expenses in their programs.

Property that had been used for missionary residences was considered to be in a different category. The Commission claimed these assets for its use in housing its personnel. Churches sometimes felt bound by the former Mission programs, for they could only assign personnel to places where there were missionary residences. We were prepared to secure housing in a new area, but we needed the money from the sale of the other properties. During the 1960s we attempted to rent housing wherever possible so that fraternal workers would be available for more flexible strategies, but this expense was greater than could be met when most economies were in the midst of heavy inflation. The exception to our rule about missionary residences being claimed by COEMAR were those cases where the residence was part of an institution, for example, faculty housing at a school or homes for the medical staff of a hospital. Such property was considered part of the institution and transferred with it.

Although our property policies seemed reasonable to us, they did not always strike the church leaders the same way. The complexities of the process were not easy to explain. Our refusal to pay the large taxes, or our concern that they have an adequate holding body, often came through to the churches as our reluctance to give them what they felt was rightfully theirs. The property problems were always present, even though we made some progress in certain countries, and we passed many of them on to the successor agencies.

Charlie Leber believed that the Commission on Ecumenical Mission and Relations should move in new directions, and he proposed that the Commission invite a group of people from other churches to advise us on next steps. This project became known as the Advisory Study. It was the last of many creative contributions Charles Leber made to the mission work of the church.

6

An Advisory Study

The idea of an Advisory Study Committee was proposed by Charlie Leber in the summer of 1958. The Commission on Ecumenical Mission and Relations had just been formed, and inviting people from other parts of the world to advise about its future seemed in keeping with its spirit. The proposal was approved by the Commission at its first meeting, and Henry Pitney Van Dusen, president of Union Theological Seminary, New York, was asked to chair a small committee that would prepare the project. I was assigned to do the preparatory staff work.

The selection of the Advisory Study Committee was the responsibility of the Commission. Not all the churches with which we were related could be represented, nor could all the ecumenical organizations in which we held membership. We informed these groups of our plans and welcomed their suggestions through personal contacts. No one, however, was asked to make an official nomination.

This approach reflects the stage of development in our ecumenical attitudes. We were not prepared to trust the selection of the participants to other churches or organizations. We wanted the advice of other people, but we controlled the selection of who would give us the advice. The size of the Advisory Study Committee, the categories of membership, and the individuals selected were entirely the decisions of a group of North American United Presbyterians.

We decided on fifteen members, two thirds of whom were to be from outside the United States. The five from the United States would include three members from the Commission and two fraternal workers under appointment by the Commission but serving in other countries. We were trying to get a committee whose members would establish its credibility and at the same time bring different perspectives. We wanted representation from the ecumenical movement, from churches with which we had been related in mission, and from some areas where we had not been involved. We needed people who had been related to the two former denominations— some lay, some clergy, some from medical ministries, some from education, and some from functional services. We wanted some who were involved with church institutions, some from the secular world, and a balance of representation from the geographical regions. This mixture was achieved in fifteen individuals.

The project required full-time staff services, and Glenn Reed was selected. He had served as a missionary in the Sudan, had been the staff leader of the United Presbyterian Board, and was then serving as Commission Representative for the Sudan and Ethiopia. He was quite aware of the policy issues involved and of the difficulty in getting churches and Missions to move in new directions. He was given leave of absence as a Commission Representative for this assignment. Ruth Shutes, who had been Charlie Leber's secretary, became his administrative assistant.

When we had selected the persons we intended to invite, we asked the Commission Representatives to share the list with church leaders in their area and to discover the acceptability of the members selected from their churches. There was a negative reaction from Brazil. One of the two fraternal workers was Dick Shaull, who was serving in Brazil in theological education, and one of the lay members was Esdras Costa, a young Brazilian sociologist. Both were active in the student movement. The Presbyterian Church of Brazil was at odds with the student movement and found neither of these persons acceptable. We felt that securing another lay sociologist from Brazil who would be acceptable to the church was almost an impossibility, and rearranging the spectrum of talents and experience in the committee would rule out other valuable members. We judged that process too difficult and decided to stick with our original proposal. In the light of later developments I believe that decision was a mistake. Each of the individuals involved made a fine contribution to the work of the committee, but the church in Brazil felt insulted, and it opposed moves we made to get the Advisory Study report used in Latin America. This tension was one of a long series that led to the break between the two denominations.

The invitations had already been extended when Charlie Leber died. The question arose as to whether we should go ahead with the proposal. Within the staff and the Commission there were a number of persons who had not been enthusiastic about the idea but had been unwilling to oppose Charlie. There were a number of lively discussions in staff, at one of the furlough conferences, and in the planning committee. In one of these exchanges a fraternal worker commented, "The Commission, like the Board before it, has the ability to set up a study process that will reach the conclusion the Commission already has in mind." It was a helpful comment, for I became determined to prove that criticism wrong.

Part of the problem was the timing. We were trying to move ahead while the selection of Charlie Leber's successor was still in process. If the new General Secretary was to be John Coventry Smith, then all would be well. If the Commission was to move outside the staff in its selection, then it would be unfair to saddle the new leader with a process intended to be quite definitive for the future. The staff, however, did recommend that we proceed.

The Commission considered this recommendation at the meeting in which it elected John Smith as General Secretary. He had to use the influence of his new status to get the recommendation approved. He pointed out that the genius of this proposal was in setting such a group free to select its own processes and to criticize the Commission if the study led in that direction.

The members of the Advisory Study Committee were an outstanding group. The chairperson was Chang Hui Hwang, principal of Tainan Theological Seminary in Taiwan. He was known as Shokie to his associates, and later changed his last name back to an earlier form. He is today widely known as Shokie Coe. A fine biblical scholar and theologian, he led the committee very well. Rafael Cepeda was a Presbyterian pastor from Cuba serving as executive secretary of the Commission on Presbyterian Cooperation in Latin America. He was sympathetic with the social goals of the Cuban revolution and remained in Cuba. Esdras Costa was a young sociology teacher from Brazil, a member of the Presbyterian Church of Brazil and active in the Student Christian Movement. Fayez Fares, a young pastor from

Egypt, had studied a year at Princeton Seminary and was one of the coming leaders of the Evangelical Church. Francis Ibiam was a medical doctor who had served in mission hospitals in Nigeria. At the time of his country's independence he was knighted and as Sir Francis Ibiam served as governor of Eastern Nigeria. During the Biafran conflict he renounced his title and became known as Dr. Akanu Ibiam. Wadad Khoury Jeha was principal of the Sidon Girls School in Lebanon, one of the church-related schools. Pyung-Kan Koh was a medical doctor and became the president of Yonsei University in Korea. Philippe Maury, a pastor of the Reformed Church in France, had been secretary of the World Student Christian Federation and was a staff member of the World Council of Churches. Matthew Ogawa, a lay leader in the United Church of Christ in Japan, was director of Audiovisual Activities for the National Christian Council. W. S. Theophilus, a lay leader in the United Church of North India, was principal of the United Christian Schools of Jullundur. Catherine Alexander, a fraternal worker serving in Iran, was a leader in the church's ministries among women. Richard Shaull had served as a missionary in Colombia before going to Brazil. Through his leadership in World Student Christian Federation programs he was known in many countries. Ada Black, a leader in United Presbyterian Women, a pastor's wife, a former member of the Board of Foreign Missions and a Commission member, had visited several countries as a member of church delegations. Richard Davies, a management consultant, lay leader in the Washington, D.C., area, was a vice-chairperson of the Commission. Robert Gibson was president of Monmouth College, a Commission member, and the former chairperson of the United Presbyterian Permanent Committee on Interchurch Relations.

Some directions were set for the committee. It is easier to tell what you do not want. We did not want them to write a "theology of missions"; there were plenty in existence. We did not expect the committee to examine all that the two former denominations had been doing in foreign missions and then make specific program suggestions. That task would be overwhelming, and there were many people more qualified than the committee members to make the specific suggestions in various areas. We did, however, ask them to work in the range of "the middle axioms," the policies and directions that form the tie between theology and programs. It is in this range that organizations become inconsistent and confusion sets in.

The Advisory Study Committee held three meetings. The first took place at the Ecumenical Training Center in Stony Point, and for two weeks the members studied the scriptures and examined various materials on mission policy. Before settling in at Stony Point, they spent two days with the staff at "475" and heard from Pitt Van Dusen and John Smith about the Commission's hopes for their work. Partway through this first meeting they spent an evening with the Commission's Committee on Policy and Strategy.

As they got into their meetings it became evident they would have to do some work in the theology of mission. They needed to establish a common viewpoint. The committee members came from such diverse backgrounds and experiences that they were talking past each other. Their theological approach, and the one that became the foundation of their report, grew out of their Bible study sessions.

Most of us who had worked on the preparation of the project had assumed that the Advisory Study would result in some recommendations to the Commission about its future directions. However, the committee members had seen too many reports "received with appreciation" and then shelved. Furthermore, as they considered the variety of situations facing the Commission, they would have neither the time nor the information to address all of them with enough clarity to be helpful. They proposed to produce a report that would raise the issues which the Commission and related churches should study together. It would be out of this second study effort, the follow-up of their work, that the Commission and related churches could agree on next steps. Therefore, the report became *An Advisory Study.*[1]

The committee members needed exposure to situations different from those out of which they came. Visits were arranged that took advantage of travel to and from their meetings. This plan saved money and also meant that the committee members gave at least a month to each meeting.

The second meeting was held in Asmara, Ethiopia. The Commission called a meeting of Commission Representatives to meet at the same time, and there was adequate opportunity for interchange. There was input from the Commission Representatives to the committee's process, and the committee members had a chance to clarify some of the impressions gained through their travels.

At the final meeting, held in Evanston, Illinois, they completed their report. A Furlough Study Conference was being held at McCormick Theological Seminary in Chicago, and it was to be followed by a Commission meeting at which the report would be presented. Fraternal workers at the conference were invited to stay for the meeting.

The Advisory Study Committee had worked out a good presentation, using all the members who were present. It was clearly the report of the whole committee, Even its style showed that different persons had prepared the various sections. It was such a full document that we could not comprehend all that it contained. However, there was such a positive response that some of the Commission members had to be reminded that the report was only to be received, not adopted. The report was to be studied with churches and ecumenical organizations. Part of the circulation process was a disclaimer that *An Advisory Study* was not to be interpreted as the policy of the Commission.

The Advisory Study Committee was dismissed with great appreciation. The members had prepared an unusual and a very useful study. They had become a community, and several lasting friendships were formed among its members. Shokie edited the document into a more polished style since it was evidently a committee product, though he kept the general style characteristics which showed that persons from several cultures had been involved in writing it.

The document was printed in English and eventually translated into twelve languages. We sent copies to a large number of churches in various parts of the world, to all member agencies of the Division of Foreign Missions of the National Council of Churches and of the Division of World Mission and Evangelism of the World Council of Churches. It was well received by many people who were struggling with its issues, and eventually more than twelve thousand copies were distributed.

The report had implications for how any church perceives its mission and carries out its witness in the world. We circulated it to all the governing bodies and agencies of our denomination and distributed copies to all commissioners at the General Assembly. However, we were not successful in getting the church to see it as something other than a report that concerned our overseas mission.

The Commission itself began immediately to study the report. Task forces were appointed to explore particular issues that emerged, and each prepared a supplementary paper. There were seven of these papers on the following issues: the church as a charismatic community, the place of Christian institutions, the role of the Commission in overseas responsibilities, missionaries in the contemporary church, the ecumenical movement as a factor in mission overseas, the responsible appropriation of funds, and factors to be considered in evaluating Christian medical work.

Since most of the material in the report had implications for the relations we had established through mission, as chairman of the Division of Ecumenical Mission I was assigned to direct the follow-up process. The specific activities covered about four years, but we were applying the results for a number of years.

The first step in the study process with related churches was to get the report introduced in an ecumenical and regional setting where its issues could be discussed on their merits. The first exposure, therefore, would be in a setting that was not just a "one on one" meeting between COEMAR and a related church. John Smith carried a hundred copies to the World Council of Churches Assembly in New Delhi and presented them to representatives of churches with which we were related. In an informal discussion he was able to introduce the report and tell people how seriously the Commission was taking it.

This World Council of Churches Assembly in New Delhi was the occasion for the merger of the International Missionary Council as the Division of World Mission and Evangelism. One of its first emphases was called Joint Action for Mission which challenged the churches to go beyond the usual forms of cooperation to joint planning and action in what they usually considered "their own work." The East Asia Christian Conference was holding three "situation conferences" on Joint Action for Mission to initiate this new approach in Asia. *An Advisory Study* raised many of the same concerns, so it was one of the major documents for the conferences. John Smith had been active in founding the East Asia Christian Conference, and he was invited to attend these situation conferences.

The Near East Christian Council called a study conference on this report and invited people from Pakistan and

India to join them. Members of the committee from the region were in attendance. The secretary of the Near East Christian Council asked me to prepare questions that would assist the small discussion groups to get into the study. The educational system of the region had not prepared people to participate in small-group discussions with questions to stimulate thought. The participants assumed they were required to come up with answers to all the questions! The conference did get the report introduced, but we did not come to grips with how churches relate in mission.

The World Presbyterian Alliance was holding a study conference for its African member churches. It agreed to our request to have *An Advisory Study* placed on the agenda. I was asked to introduce the study, so I wrote a précis and delivered it as a speech. We were able to have the report presented and some of its issues discussed, even though it was not the main theme of the conference.

The summary I had prepared seemed to help people get an understanding of *An Advisory Study,* so the Commission printed it as one of a series of Significant Papers and gave it wide circulation under the title "Captives in Christ's Triumphal Procession."

The Commission on Presbyterian Cooperation in Latin America, an organization that grew out of North American Mission activities, was holding a study conference in Chile. We were members of that group, and its executive committee was quite willing to put *An Advisory Study* on the agenda. Unfortunately the Spanish translation was delayed, and I had to carry copies with me to the conference. Few of the participants had examined it.

When the agenda of the conference was being presented in the first session, the representatives of the Presbyterian Church of Brazil protested *An Advisory Study* being on the agenda and threatened to walk out if it was kept there. So we made no presentation of the document itself. It may be that the curiosity of other members was piqued, wondering what was so terrible about the document. However, we were beginning to pay the penalty for how we had selected the Brazilian member of the committee.

Following this conference we had a meeting with the church in Chile to discuss the possibility of a time when we together could examine *An Advisory Study* and discover its implications for our relationship. Two pastors from Brazil were serving as fraternal workers with the church in

Chile, and they tried to block the proposal, saying that their church would not want them to participate in a discussion of that document. The Chileans were incensed at this interference with their independence and made it clear that they would make their own decision in this matter. They agreed upon a study consultation with COEMAR.

These various regional events completed the first stage of the follow-up process. We were moving into the second stage of direct conversations with the churches. Since we were dealing with the regions as units in the study, there was an overlap of the two stages. Some of the direct negotiations were under way in Asia before the regional events had been completed in other areas.

In dealing with this Advisory Study follow-up, we faced a problem related to our ecumenical style. We had proposed the study because COEMAR was a new-style organization and we wanted advice about its future. However, some of our problems were common to all mission agencies, and we should have invited other agencies to join the project. There was the dilemma. If we opened the project to other groups, there would be delays while they decided whether or not to join. Also, the scope of the project might become so broad that it would not address COEMAR's unique problems. On the other hand, if we did not invite others to join, we were denying our ecumenical commitment to some extent, and we might face difficulty in implementing recommendations. We chose to keep the project within COEMAR's control, and it was in this problem of implementing findings that we discovered our difficulties. We were quite involved with these other agencies in our mission work, and in some countries the follow-up depended on their cooperation. We were faced with trying to persuade them to join us in the study of a document that they had not helped to prepare. We hoped that other groups would agree to study the document on the merit of its material, and many people were prepared to salute its ideas. They were not prepared to enter into some study process just because the United Presbyterians wanted to hammer out their future policy.

In Japan, Hong Kong, and the Philippines our channel of communication with the churches was through an Interboard Committee for each country. These committees coordinated the work of the North American mission agencies working with those churches. The three committees had one full-time executive. The Interboard Committee Office was related to, but not a part of, the Division of Foreign Missions of the National Council of Churches. Although these were staff committees, composed of the regional secretaries of the agencies, they really functioned as small mission boards for the work in these countries. It was impossible for us to have discussions on *An Advisory Study* in these three countries until the request had been cleared through the Interboard Committee; one mission agency could not examine its relationship with one of the churches without involving the others. We were not able to persuade the committees that such discussions were important for us, and COEMAR had to settle for raising some of the issues in other meetings that were being scheduled. *An Advisory Study* had little effect on our activities in those countries.

A similar problem confronted us in our relations with the Presbyterian Church U.S. In Mexico, Brazil, Korea, Taiwan, and Japan the two denominations were involved with the same church. Yet we had not invited their Board of World Missions to join us in establishing the committee. Darby Fulton, their chief executive, held views on mission policy that were almost at the opposite pole from Charlie Leber's. Watson Street, his successor, was much more sympathetic to our viewpoint, but he did not come on the scene until the Advisory Study Committee was well along with its work. In 1962 the Board of World Missions called a major policy consultation at Montreat, North Carolina. It involved board members, representatives of overseas churches, missionaries, and representatives of ecumenical organizations in a process of setting future directions. The report of this consultation was as important to their future as *An Advisory Study* was to ours. The documents were different in style, but both influenced the agenda of discussions with the churches to which the two denominations were related.

The conversations with the particular churches to which we were related in mission were filled with tension. They obviously were the prelude to some sort of change. The coemar representatives were committed to entering the discussions with no preconceived notions about what the changes would be. We knew that some basic policy issues were at stake, so Commission and staff members made up the delegations. As the discussions proceeded, we expected to indicate the direction the changes might take. To provide continuity in the follow-up, I attended most of the consultations.

The concern that took most of our attention was that of breaking the patterns of dependence. The integration of the Missions into the churches had been a transfer of power, and some of that power had been transferred to New York. The new arrangements worked out in some situations had made the church even more dependent on COEMAR than it had been in Mission days.

An example of this problem was what happened in the church in Colombia. It was a small Presbyterian denomination of fewer than five thousand members. It was organized as a synod with three presbyteries. It had no administrative staff. Any correspondence with the United Presbyterian Church was through the Mission, which did have a full-time secretary.[2] The Mission was being dissolved and its responsibilities transferred to the church. The synod felt it would need an executive secretary, but it could not afford one. The Commission agreed to grant funds to the synod so it could have such an officer, but the synod must select the person. The church leaders wanted to be sure their new relationships were carried on responsibly; they were anxious to select someone who would have the confidence of the Commission and of the former missionaries who were becoming fraternal workers. After a number of informal contacts a man was selected. He was soon branded as the missionaries' choice and as New York's man. Even after efforts to correct the process in the selection of his successor, the impression remained that while COEMAR supplied the money, it would have a powerful influence on what the executive did.

One of the most extreme examples of the dependence syndrome was in northern India. The church members were from the former outcaste group of that society. They were very poor, and small groups were scattered through many rural villages. None of the groups were large enough to be called congregations. The Mission had provided pastoral care for these groups by employing evangelists, men who had been given a Bible school level training after a primary or middle school education. In one of the synods this network of rural worshiping groups plus a few larger congregations, usually located next to some larger Mission institution, constituted the church. Most of the lay leadership in that synod were teachers, doctors, nurses, and other persons employed in the Mission institutions. When the Mission was dissolved and the church took over responsibility, the church's leaders were practically all dependent on a Mission program that had been directed and financed by the Americans. As one Advisory Committee member remarked, "You did not integrate the Mission into the church, you integrated with an association of your own employees." In the follow-up process we discovered the truth of that observation. The former "evangelists" were called "rural pastors," and their salaries still came from New York through a grant to the synod. But the rural pastors were not aware of any change, and in the discussions they kept reminding the COEMAR representatives that they were our employees. This one synod in northern India was the extreme problem, but some elements were to be found in the churches in India and Pakistan.

It was during this follow-up process that I came to see how one image common in mission circles was almost demonic in its perpetuation of the dependence spirit. It is the mother-daughter image applied to churches that grew out of the foreign mission work. Even *An Advisory Study* fell into the trap of using it. "The terms 'mother' and 'daughter' applied to churches are used in the Report as the most convenient possible means of indicating a relationship between two churches when one church has shared in the origin of another."[3] The image is theologically unsound and is damaging to both parties.

My rejection of the image came during my discussions with the church in India. This is a church that came into existence in spite of missionary policy, not because of it. The early missionaries confronted a tightly structured caste system which permitted no social mobility. They decided to aim for the upper levels of the caste system, feeling sure that converts among these people would communicate the gospel to the other castes and that the impact of the Christians would eventually destroy the system. That statement is an oversimplification of how some very devoted people tried to witness in the face of such a tightly structured system. However, when the first outcastes, from the very lowest level of the social system, appeared for baptism they touched off a debate in the missionary community. The missionaries knew that a church composed of outcastes would find difficulty in witnessing to the higher levels of society. However, they felt they could not deny baptism when there was evidence that the Holy Spirit had been at work, the outcastes were baptized, and the future of the church was set.

A mass movement into the Christian faith from the outcaste groups occurred a few years later. There were large numbers of illiterate converts to be helped. The missionaries began to prepare these new Christians to become a church: self-propagating, self-governing, and self-supporting. Schools were founded, teachers were trained, Bible camps taught the scriptures by rote, Bible schools prepared evangelists and Bible women, and a seminary prepared ministerial candidates. District missionaries supervised evangelists and village schools, and encouraged rural congregations. Two generations later this church was dependent on that Mission program. No one intended it to happen; the dependence was the result of the good intentions of committed people somehow going awry.

If ever there was a church that should remind us that conversion is the work of the Holy Spirit, it is the church in northern India and Pakistan. But in the 1950s the church members there were referring to the church that sent them missionaries as "the mother church." If ever there was a church that should have known that its life was rooted in God, it should have been the church in northern India and Pakistan. But when it needed something, it looked to New York as the source of all help.

When I realized what had happened, I was angry. I had enjoyed my role as a representative of "the mother church." The United Presbyterian Church had easily slipped into the role of "mother" and had treated the church in India and Pakistan with the benevolent condescension due immature children. We were willing to be needed when resources were required, had been happy to be appreciated when they were sent, and in blithe arrogance had happily supplanted God in their lives. The image was as damaging to the United Presbyterians as it was to the dignity of the church in Pakistan and India. I prepared a speech called "Don't Call Me Mother!" and served notice that we wanted out of a relationship that destroyed our spiritual sensitivity.

We finally decided that the way out was to remove all subsidies for church programs in northern India and Pakistan. This decision was made after long and difficult negotiations. The subsidies that we planned to withdraw affected every part of the church structure. The synod executive, the district superintendents (who had replaced the former district missionaries), and the pastors were all affected. There were also a number of projects, such as "promotion of audiovisual programs" and "rural church improvement," which were not fulfilling their original purpose. To continue these projects, which provided salaries, would only cause internal tension over competition for the jobs.

We were accused of destroying the church, but what we had discovered was a facade, a duplication of the former Mission structure. No one could tell whether a real community of believers was contained in it or not. The church had never examined what sort of structure was appropriate for India. If, after a hundred years of mission work in that part of India, the church could be destroyed by a budget act from New York, then we should admit our failure and let the church in India assume responsibility for establishing a witness in that area. We did not believe the Mission had failed, we believed that a church would emerge. If it proved to be weak, the rest of the church in that country could strengthen it. The system we were supporting seemed to perpetuate its weakness.

The negotiations then centered on the method of withdrawing financial support. Through the years there had been a number of efforts to reduce subsidies slowly and to eliminate them eventually, but always on the assumption that the system would be continued through support raised in India. Such plans were always abandoned because the church in India could not pick up the support. Our plan was not to continue the system but to eliminate it and let the church in India devise its own method of supporting a ministry. We proposed to withdraw support in two years.

The final arrangement was to give the people involved a notice of almost a year plus a terminal grant of two years' salary. Most of the pastors were in debt to the local money lender, and this grant could free them of this burden while giving them a sum to invest in some income-producing activity such as raising poultry. Some of the rural congregations wanted to keep their pastors, and this time period gave them an opportunity to work out support for them.

During the period of these negotiations the Punjab, a wheat-growing area known as "the breadbasket of India," experienced what was known in southern Asia as "the green revolution." A new wheat strain that gave a much larger yield per acre was introduced. The Punjab was suddenly prosperous. In our final discussions the church leaders were sure the congregations could support their pastors and some of the programs. The tone of our discussions changed from tension to cooperation within twelve months. It was an interesting lesson on the psychological power of economic improvement.

Not long after the Commission implemented its India actions, the United Church of North India merged with several other churches to form the Church of North India. This church is episcopal in structure and has a different system of pastoral support. It is a strong church and has recognized its responsibility for the work in the former North India Synod.

One of the approaches we developed in the follow-up process was to study what is essential to being a church. Some of the churches that had been overshadowed by well-organized Missions felt that schools and hospitals were a necessary part of a church. They felt they would never truly be the church in their country until they controlled these institutions. However, in some countries new governments were taking over all former Mission schools, and the churches were still able to operate. Our purpose in this discussion was to identify those things which are essential to a church and then to identify those things which are helpful to its ministries. We then argued that a denomination must be in control of the essentials if it is to be in control of its own life. Control means support as well, for if another church provides the finances, it can cripple an essential activity by withdrawing funds.

Our list of essentials usually included worship, study of the scriptures, teaching the faith to the next generation, selecting and ordaining ministers, maintaining organizational structure, and witnessing to the faith in society. It was our position that none of the money we supplied should be used for these activities. If a church could not afford to hold a General Assembly every year, then it should hold one as often as it could afford to do so. If a church could not afford a full-time executive, then it should work out other ways of running the organization. By taking such steps, a church could feel free of any domination of its life as a church.

We wrote a policy paper on "Partnership in Mission"[4]

which set forth this idea of not influencing the central life of another church. We were prepared to work with a church in developing its church life but not in supporting it. We were prepared to join in those activities which the church used in its mission to the society of which it was a part. Each church must be free to control its own life and also to decide on the things it wants to do with help from another church. After each consultation we prepared a paper that spelled out the specific agreements with a particular church. For example, we prepared a paper "Partnership in Mission with the United Church of North India."

This process of negotiation was an attempt to set churches free. In one of our staff meetings I made that comment, and a colleague challenged me with the question, "Free from what?" My reply was: "Free from us! *An Advisory Study* .claimed that the mission enterprise had tied those churches to the United Presbyterian Church and that Mission-church integration had not really loosened those ties. We must set them free from our control."

In some cases we would achieve this goal of their freedom only by declaring our own independence. As we have indicated earlier, some of the churches felt they had a proprietary interest in our activity in their part of the world. Sometimes this impression was the result of certain administrative practices held over from the Mission structure. For example, under the Mission structure we made budget allocations by countries—a certain amount for Egypt, for Iran, and so on. It was the Mission's job to administer the budget within its program. If the Board found it necessary to reduce budgets, an unwritten agreement resulted in a percentage cut applied to all Missions. After the Mission-church integration we discovered that the same attitude persisted: the churches were protesting any cut from one year to the next unless we explained that we were cutting all church allocations on a proportionate scale.

This proprietary interest has also been referred to when we attempted to relate to another church in the same country. The church with which we had been traditionally working sometimes took offense but also reminded us that our relations with different groups in their country could raise the local tension level. We tried to be sensitive in such situations, but we still maintained our responsibility to be open to many contacts.

As we declared our own freedom to explore new contacts, we urged the related churches to do the same. Many of them were becoming members of the major ecumenical and confessional organizations and would have the opportunity to make new "partners in mission" through such contacts. That freedom was exercised. In some cases the relationship was with independent organizations that appeared on the scene offering help—for example, World Vision and Campus Crusade. In other cases the new contacts were with churches in Europe.

Another step in helping a church sense its freedom was to reduce both financial contributions and the number of fraternal worker personnel to the point where we could not have a determinative effect in the life of the other church. In some countries the United Presbyterian Church had a large missionary contingent, which could exercise considerable power in a small church. In some cases the process of reduction was worked out with the churches involved. In other cases the Commission was taking arbitrary action, not always justified. Vacancies through retirements and registrations were not filled. As some fraternal workers felt their work had reached the limits of usefulness, the Commission shifted them to other countries. This deliberate reduction of our influence in the life of another church was difficult to interpret—difficult in the related church where only a few leaders understood the strategy, difficult in the United Presbyterian Church where the members had been educated to believe that their contributions made a great difference to the churches in other countries.

The fact that we were responsible for ecumenical relations opened new opportunities. We could discover places for capable persons who needed to be moved. We were willing to help in many places, but in no place were we to be so strong that our withdrawal would cripple a church. The strategy was a deliberate dispersal of power.

The entire process covered almost eight years: half the lifetime of COEMAR. It was a determinative time for many churches. The work of the Advisory Study Committee was a great factor in shaping the mission activity of the United Presbyterian Church.

7

Changes in the Role and the Support of Missionaries

The foreign mission enterprise was embodied in the missionary. Over more than a century of mystique surrounded these people who left their homes and families, sacrificed comfort and careers to live and work in often dangerous circumstances as a response to God's special calling. The calling was both personal and corporate. The missionaries volunteered in response to a feeling that God had called them personally, and the church appointed and supported them in response to a sense that God called his church to certain mission responsibilities. The measure of faithfulness in mission was the number of people a church sent to the mission frontiers either in this nation or abroad.

The church thus created an elite corps of workers, the missionaries, and loaded on them the burden of witnessing to its best understanding of the gospel. The church in general was far from perfect, but the feeling was that the church's major imperfections would be filtered out of the foreign and home missionary work. To some extent the missionary community met these expectations. Everyone received the same income in what was a support system of low basic salary with additional allowances according to need. They had concepts of equal participation in decision-making long before the term participatory democracy was known. Women held equal status in the Missions at a very early time. None of these arrangements were perfect, for the people were shaped by their cultures. But there was a sense in which their commitment, style, and efforts were ahead of the rest of the church.

Following World War II the missionaries were paying the price of success. The church existed in almost every nation, and Western Christians had to change their understanding of the place missionary personnel played in the

mission of the whole church. No longer could a denomination measure its effectiveness in mission by counting the
number of missionaries under appointment.

The Presbyterian Board had started to use the term "ecumenical personnel" when it began to use the term "ecumenical mission." Not only was it trying to set the new
context for the American personnel it would be appointing,
it was recognizing that the missionary forces would be
recruited from many nations.

One effort to enlarge participation in the missionary task
was the encouragement of related churches to send out
their own missionaries. This was not a new idea. The
churches of Korea had sent missionaries into China in the
early part of the century, and there were other examples in
Asia. However, churches that were not yet self-supporting
were reluctant to divert resources to such a program. At
the same time, it seemed important that the missionary
force reflect the ecumenical nature of the church, deliver
the mission enterprise from being Western dominated, and
show that the whole church was taking the whole gospel to
the whole world. We tried to establish a framework in
which a church in Asia or Africa or Latin America could
supply personnel with part of their support and a church
in North America or Europe could provide the rest of the
financial needs.

We met several problems in our attempt to implement
this program. One was the transfer of funds. The international monetary system was based on the dollar, and in
countries that had a negative balance of payments it was
difficult for the church to get permission to send money
out of the country. Sometimes the only way the church's
support could reach a worker was through transfers worked
out with COEMAR. The result was that a Filipino nurse working in Iran might get all her money through the financial
channels of COEMAR. It was hard to convince the church in
Iran that she was not working for COEMAR, and the relationship between the church in Iran and the church in the
Philippines did not develop.

Another problem arose around the communication lines
in arranging such appointments. Sometimes we initiated a
specific idea and were directly involved in getting the
invitation from one church delivered to another. The
Commission's consultant in urban mission proposed that a
Japanese pastor be sent to Cairo, and even helped recruit

the pastor. Correspondence went through the Commission Representative in Egypt. The project was seen both in Japan and in Egypt as a COEMAR project, not a relationship between the churches in Egypt and Japan. Our Regional Secretary for Latin America suggested to the church in Chile that it invite the church in Brazil to send some personnel. When tze Chileans agreed, he then carried the invitation to Brazil. We were helping finance the project and should have sent our contribution to Brazil as a sign that we were helping the Brazilian church respond to the call from Chile. However, international transfer procedures and national exchange regulations made it more convenient for us to send our money directly to Chile, which only strengthened the impression that these particular Brazilians were working for the United Presbyterian Church. In a discussion some two years later in Brazil we discovered the misunderstanding. The Brazilian church insisted it had recruited these workers to help its friends in the United Presbyterian Church U.S.A; its own mission priorities would not have led it to send someone to work in Chile.

Another problem arose because the local framework in which these people would work had been developed by the American missionaries. The church in Egypt was excited over sending one of its best young pastors, Rev. Swailem Sidholm, as a missionary to the South Sudan. However, Swailem and his family had to live in a mission compound built for Americans and had to fit into a life-style of that mission community. The church in Egypt gave Swailem a bicycle for transportation, but the Americans had jeeps. The school for missionary children prepared students for the American school system, not the Egyptian. Similar problems arose in Thailand when people from Japan, Korea, and the Philippines were invited to work with the church. They were assigned housing that had belonged to the Mission, their children had to go to the International School in Bangkok, and the entire venture was far more expensive than any of the churches had anticipated. These workers also discovered that some of the benefits of the extended family, the social pattern out of which they had come, were not available to them in this strange land. One church leader in Latin America said that the experience of trying to support some of their pastors who had been sent to another country had given him much more sympathy for some of the problems the Americans working with his own church had faced.

Mission agencies worked together to solve these problems, and what we know as "three-way mission" still continues. However, none of these programs expanded as fast as we thought they would. Some of the problems would have been minimized through an ecumenical approach, and we were one agency that pressed the World Council of Churches to pick up the activity. This effort is described in the next chapter.

We have described earlier the way in which the Mission organizations, which were the power base of the American missionaries, had been integrated into the churches and how the term "missionary" was changed to "fraternal worker." The change symbolized a different status; these people would now work alongside their Christian brothers and sisters in the mission of the church. It meant a shift in the focus of relationships. When I first became involved in mission administration, the focus of concern was on how well a missionary was able to relate to other missionaries. At the end of a missionary's first term the Mission voted on whether a missionary should be returned after furlough. There were numerous articles and books about the importance of such relationships and the effect they had on Christian witness. In the new situation the emphasis shifted to the relationships the fraternal workers had with administrators and colleagues in the churches.

When churches became responsible for inviting and assigning fraternal workers, some method had to be developed for helping the church assess the effective work of the personnel and their relations with church colleagues. This task was far more difficult than it appeared at first. Most of the cultures in which these churches existed had no way of dealing with this sort of question. The idea of a personnel committee was beyond their experience. Our requests for job descriptions and personnel evaluations were an example of how the integration process in some ways was more of a Western domination of the church than the old mission structures; we were forcing them into our style of doing things in order to meet our administrative needs.

The loss of the Mission structure created more personnel problems than we had anticipated. In the Mission there had been a personal and pastoral concern for new missionaries. A senior missionary couple were assigned to help new

arrivals through the first months, and a language committee provided orientation to the culture as well as the language. The Mission meeting once a year provided both
fellowship and inspiration. A station meeting gave guidance in fulfilling tasks assigned. This structure was all
dismantled, and many of these activities the church had no
way of duplicating. Few church leaders had been given the
opportunity to learn of the problems faced by expatriates
living in their country.

Colombia was one of the places where COEMAR faced
some of its most difficult relations involving fraternal workers, the church, and the Commission. The mission work
had developed churches in three different areas of the
country, and each of them became a presbytery in the
synod. However, it was the structure of the Mission that
provided the communication and administrative network
for this church. The synod held its annual meetings, but
there was little communication among the presbyteries
themselves. There was not much sense of unity as a synod.

Colombia as a nation was passing through one of the
most difficult periods of its history, a ten-year period of
violence when civil authority broke down and internal
conflicts led to the death of almost a half million people.
That atmosphere in the society had its effect on relationships within the church.

When the Mission was integrated into the church, the
Mission as an organization went out of existence. The
synod established an office of executive secretary, but it
was a new experience for all concerned. The synod secretary had a small budget, no staff, and no experience in what
was needed to make a new system function well.

The fraternal workers were thrown into a new situation
in which the lines of authority over their work were not
clear. There was no support structure to meet personnel
needs, and therefore a growing level of frustration and
anxiety developed. Two consultations were initiated by
COEMAR with the synod to clarify some of the problems, for
the synod was also trying to understand its responsibilities
for programs that formerly were controlled by the Mission
and supported by COEMAR. In each case the representatives
from COEMAR raised the problem of the relations with fraternal workers, and specific proposals were agreed upon,
in one case a personnel committee with representatives of
the fraternal workers on it. What we failed to work out

were the specific steps by which such agreements would
be implemented, and there was no follow-through. What
was frustrating from the Commission's viewpoint was that
we were constantly being blamed for our decisions in
Colombia, but we were not making such decisions! The
tensions finally became so difficult that we sent someone
to perform a pastoral ministry with the fraternal workers.
He made recommendations which we accepted and which
helped ease the tensions.

I have used this country as an illustration of what happens when new situations set people adrift professionally
and personally. Each of the countries in which we went
through such integration had this problem to some degree.

Several months after we had been struggling with this
problem in Colombia, we had a psychologist address the
home assignment conference. He had been one of the
leaders in the orientation work at the center in Stony Point,
and our personnel staff had called on him to help with
certain problems that faced the people on furlough. In his
lecture he placed a dot in the center of a blackboard. "This
dot represents a person," he said, "but the person never
stands bare. The person always defines the self in terms of
reference points." He then surrounded the dots with the
traditional reference points of the missionary: American,
member of a Mission, a decision maker, probably white,
one who controls funds, a director of a school or a hospital,
and so on. He then showed how these reference points
were disappearing in the world of the 1960s: being an
American was a liability, in some areas being white was a
detriment, decision-making power and control of funds
had been transferred to churches, and the missionary was
no longer assigned as the director of the school or the
hospital. The missionary as a person was stripped of reference points. "And do you know what this person does?"
asked the psychologist. "He gets mad at headquarters. He
thinks that '475' has let him down, he believes that no one
in the Commission cares what he is doing or appreciates
him." Into my mind flashed the picture of Colombia and
the tensions we had felt directed toward us. It was this sort
of problem we were dealing with in many parts of the
world.

Where there was a Commission Representative, he
assumed some of the responsibilities and tried to get support committees established, even if they were a perpetu-

ation of the former Mission groups. These arrangements were supposed to be interim until the churches could work out their own patterns, but they were often seen as attempts of the missionaries to hold on to old ways. In several consultations we asked the church to assume certain responsibilities, and the agreement that they would do these things was recorded in the findings of the meeting, but time after time there was no follow-through. We started with simple requests such as having the church leaders meet new personnel and introduce them to the country. The new personnel should see the place in which they were to work through the eyes of church leaders, not through the eyes of other missionaries. It seldom happened. Either the church leaders felt insecure in performing the task or felt it was not important.

Another function we asked the church to arrange was an annual retreat for the fraternal worker personnel. It was needed to provide the inspiration and fellowship that had been a part of Mission meetings. If the church would call such a meeting, participate in the planning, and have church personnel present, it would not be a perpetuation of the old Mission activity. But the churches seldom assumed that responsibility. In some countries the fraternal workers organized such retreats to meet their psychological and spiritual needs, and in other countries the fraternal workers waited until the church would act, a wait of several years.

Missionaries were expected to take a vacation each year, and in many countries the Mission had a vacation spot to which families could get away for a rest. In the integration process these properties were kept for the exclusive use of fraternal worker personnel. The compromises in many such arrangements were the result of COEMAR's pastoral concern for the missionary personnel who were having to make the adjustments required by the new policies. The missionaries were working their way out of a life-style established in the colonial era when Westerners were learning to survive in a culture radically different from their own. Mission compounds were an enclave of homes and work centers, intended to protect property and health; they became retreats from the pressures of unfamiliar customs and language. Houses with high ceilings made the tropics endurable; they also symbolized wealth which many local church people did not possess.

Missionaries themselves raised the issues of life-style long before integration intensified the problem. They felt that compound life separated them from the people with whom they were to identify. Several tried experiments in simple living and secured housing outside the compounds. The possibility became more available as the major urban centers offered more Western-style housing, but in reality the culture was changing to that with which the missionary was familiar. The problem of the life-style and its implications for Christian witness were not solved to anyone's satisfaction. People learned to live with it.

We have described the Study Fellowship and the Ecumenical Training Center at Stony Point in chapter 3. Their purposes were to help the new appointees understand the new day into which they were going. Don Smith and his co-workers had done a good job of developing an orientation program.

Some interdenominational efforts had been made in such orientation. The Division of Foreign Missions (DFM) of the National Council of Churches held summer sessions on the campus of Allegheny College in Pennsylvania. When others saw the value of what was happening in the longer sessions at Stony Point, an interdenominational group started to explore similar ventures. The first discussions indicated that whatever they did, it would not be like Stony Point! It is very difficult to admit that a group, like the Presbyterians, who had launched out on their own, might have been right. The Commission experienced the same difficulty when other groups went their own way.

The Commission staff were in the delicate position of wanting to invite the new group to join the effort at Stony Point but knowing that putting the invitation in those terms would kill the possibility. As members of the Division of Foreign Missions we participated in the discussions, but almost as observers. We did relate our experience and pointed out why we wanted an orientation program and not an academic degree course.

The president of Hartford Seminary really wanted the group to go there. The Kennedy School of Missions was located there, and it had been used for pre-field and furlough study by many mission agencies before the Study Fellowship was organized. The Presbyterians held the first Study Fellowship there, but found the problems of adjusting to the school schedule too great. When the DFM committee met the faculty at Hartford, it became evident that the school could not entertain an activity that was not working toward a degree. There was some concern that the seminary would endanger its accreditation if it sponsored such a program. The DFM committee then declared itself ready to discuss an arrangement with COEMAR.

John Smith tried to make the discussions easy for the DFM group. He took the position that we were willing to abandon our program at Stony Point and join with other agencies in setting up a missionary orientation program that would be satisfactory to all. The staff were on notice that they might not be retained. We even offered to sell the property to the interdenominational group of which we would now be a part.

The offer was accepted. Ted Romig, Don Smith, and I participated in the negotiations for COEMAR, and the Missionary Orientation Center came into being with eight agencies forming the corporation. A portion of the Gilmor-Sloane property was sold to it. New buildings were added, and for a few years the center trained over two hundred appointees annually. I was asked to serve as chairperson of the first board for the center.

One of the prices COEMAR had to pay was the loss of Don Smith as director of the center. The other groups, and especially the Methodist representatives, wanted a program that would have academic standing, and they wanted a director with advanced degrees. Don Smith did not have these qualifications. Also, it would be hard for them to believe that they had a new program as long as the old director was in charge. We asked Don to accept a new assignment. It later seemed ironic that, after failing to attract the people whom we felt combined academic standing with an understanding of our plans, we settled on a Methodist who lacked the advanced degrees.

The shift turned out to be a great blessing for the United Presbyterians. Ted Romig was anxious to give up his work in personnel, and John Weir, who had come from India to be South Asia Regional Secretary, was retiring. Ted Romig was happy to move into that office, and Don Smith became Secretary for Personnel. We redefined the personnel task to include responsibility for personnel development. I did not realize what a new move this was until I talked with personnel people from other boards. They were confined to recruitment and some pre-field orientation, while our assignment included concern for the career development of people under appointment.

One cooperative venture of the 1960s involved missionary recruitment. The enthusiasm of the growing churches in the 1950s and a new sense of world responsibility in America produced more people interested in overseas mission than the churches could possibly appoint. Interest does not always result in commitment, but it does generate considerable paperwork in replying to letters. The churches overseas were asking for specialists, and their governments were granting visas only to highly trained persons. The mission agencies were receiving contacts from persons whose qualifications matched none of the requests on their personnel lists but which might match a position on another list. All contacts had to be given careful attention, for the most needed person might be among them. Furthermore, someone who has just taken a serious step of spiritual and vocational commitment should not be brushed off.

The Office of Personnel Recruitment Overseas (OPRO), supported by several agencies, brought together information about the needs of related churches and about mission volunteers available. It received all letters of inquiry and tried to lead those who had more than casual interest to the agency that could best use their talents. The staff were soon dealing with almost four thousand initial contacts a year.

The idea was good and the plan worked. We were almost a decade late in trying it. Five years after it started, declining budgets reduced appointments to the minimum, and such an office became too expensive to maintain.

Don Smith gave COEMAR good leadership as we worked our way through many problems that the changing world was sending in our direction. During the mid-1960s these efforts resulted in two policy shifts. The first was stated in a paper on "The Stewardship of Human Resources."[1] It linked leadership development for the churches to the assignment of fraternal worker personnel. As churches planned their leadership development requests, they and COEMAR should see whether such trained people would replace fraternal workers. Such planning might require a new assignment in the same country, it might require relocation to another area. Such planning might also require budget shifts so the church could adequately pay the person who was being trained for greater responsibility. The paper recognized the need for the pastoral care of missionary/fraternal worker personnel as well as the need for career development. The increasing possibility of short-term contributions by volunteers and specialists was also recognized.

The next step was a paper on "The Development and Deployment of Missionary/Fraternal Worker Personnel"[2] directed to their specific problems mentioned in the earlier paper. It outlined a personnel development program, picked up on a salary review study, instituted a term appointment system, and established some job security for people over forty. These issues involved some of the most basic changes.

The image that most people held of a missionary was set by the past. The missionary had committed his or her life to service in a foreign country, would live there on a minimum income, would return occasionally on furlough, and would finally come back to retire on a minimum pension. The support patterns related to this image were built on the assumption that if health and competence held up, the missionary would spend a career in such service. Although the Boards did appoint some "short-termers" for teaching and special assignments, by far the majority of the personnel were considered "career missionaries." The church, through its mission board, accepted the responsibility of supporting them. Field salaries were set at a "living allowance" for a particular country. Other needs were met as they arose: an additional allowance for each child, school fees for children on the field and college allowance when they were of age, medical costs, and vacation allowance. An outfit allowance helped meet clothing and household needs on departure for the field, and a reoutfit allowance helped meet the costs of replacement. Any missionary who saved money had learned to be frugal. Missionaries were entered in the pension fund on the basis of their field salary, and on retirement the Board supplemented the accumulated benefits so that they reached the minimum pension. Having spent their lives on a minimum income, they could retire on a minimum pension!

The new day in mission forced a change in much of that pattern. Military conflicts in many regions, the rapidly changing political situations, and the changing role of the churches all meant that one could no longer assume a career in the mission field. It was assumed after World War II that the new missionaries would all be specialists, sent to perform a specific task, expected to teach others to do that work. In the new day, missionary service would be in short-term assignments.

The Commission revised its personnel system into term assignments. People were no longer appointed on the assumption that they would spend a career in this sort of work, although such long-term service could happen through regular reappointments. We also assumed, however, that the normal length of service would be more than one term. We established a pattern where the church and the Commission would review the service and the need for the fraternal worker at the end of every term.

It became evident that the sending church had more responsibility for its personnel than that of placing them in another church and expecting that organization to deal with all their needs. Also, if there was to be a shift of assignment between terms, the Commission had some responsibility in the preparation for the shift. Therefore we instituted a plan for personnel development interviews. They were a comprehensive review of the fraternal worker's service and personal situation, attempting to identify any anticipated turns in the person's career path and recommending study programs or other appropriate activity. The interviews were held on the field by someone with an objective viewpoint, sometimes a Commission Representative from a neighboring country and sometimes a counselor sent from the States. We eventually appointed two couples to spend full time in personnel work among the fraternal workers.

The changes in terms also required a review of the salary system. The system of a low base salary with allowances had worked for those people who stayed under appointment, but those who had resigned after ten or fifteen years of service had children about to go to college with no allowances available. We confronted a complex support system that had some contradictory assumptions and was a patchwork of numerous revisions and adjustments.

A basic change had taken place under the Board of Foreign Missions. The idea of a living allowance as a field salary sounds all right, but the amount is difficult to set. The people who made up the mission force in a particular country had a variety of spending habits, and they could not agree on what they really needed. Furthermore, who had set the idea that a foreign missionary must live in poverty?

Someone devised a formula that tied the missionary base salary to the average of all the pastors' salaries in the denomination. This information was available from the Pension Board. The formula was still one of low base salary and several allowances, but the overall income was equivalent to that of the pastor with the average salary in the denomination. This formula was one of convenience; there were no longer the tense discussions about what the base should be in a particular country. Also, the Foreign Board could now defend its treatment of the missionary/fraternal workers.

The radical nature of this change did not come out until much later. We had moved a step from what was basically a support system to a salary system, but we were still trying to blend the two. Several religious orders have followed the support system and defended it in court as a valid system of compensation, and many Christian groups are attracted to it as an expression of equality in Christ.

Tying the base salary to the average of the pastors' salaries presents some problems. This part of the budget must be increased as pastors' salaries increase, regardless of what is happening to the organization's income. Sometimes congregations would raise their pastor's salary and cut mission giving, thus increasing our expenses and reducing our income. The average of salaries seemed to be raised too high by a few large salaries in big churches and in the national agencies. We finally settled on the median salary instead of the average.

Until this salary review was undertaken, no recognition was given for long and loyal service. A new appointee just out of seminary would immediately receive income equal to the median of all pastors' salaries, the same as someone under appointment for several terms. As a result of this review, the starting level was 90 percent of the median and the top level was 115 percent.

Since people were not expecting to spend an entire career in this work, we reduced or eliminated many of the allowances and paid more cash salary. We tried to eliminate the paternalistic aspects of the system and give people more responsibility for their own affairs. Banking and shopping facilities were now available in most major urban centers of the world, and we eliminated many of the purchasing and financial services that had been necessary in an earlier era.

Mission organizations had been able to keep their institutions staffed by constantly shifting people to cover the vacancies caused by furloughs. When these institutions were transferred to the churches, there was no assurance that the number of fraternal workers would be enough to cover such problems. Furthermore, the institutions were expected to have balanced budgets. When the fraternal worker was present, it was the same as a financial subsidy, for COEMAR was paying the salary. When furlough time came and a local worker was hired to fill the vacancy, it was a financial drain on the institution's budget. We proposed that each institution pay the equivalent cost for a local worker to the fraternal worker, and COEMAR would pay the additional costs. In this way the institution was free to plan its program without trying to get a subsidy in the form of a fraternal worker. Our personnel would be accepted for their professional contribution, not their financial one. There were many problems getting this plan instituted, most of them the result of inertia. It meant a change in the way of doing things. However, it was good that we had the plan, for when COEMAR faced a financial crisis, several institutions began to pay for the personnel they wanted.

Some of the contradictions built into our system were revealed when we faced the problem of women's rights. We had always appointed both husband and wife, though we were usually looking for the professional abilities of the husband. One of the assumptions was that the couple would remain married; divorce was cause for resignation. Wives became members of the Mission, voted at its meetings, and were assigned duties. Although those were liberal steps in a time when the church would not ordain women as elders or clergy, they were also about the limit of the progress. The base salary I have mentioned above was set for a couple; married missionaries were the norm. Single people were paid a salary that was half that of a married couple. No one thought of setting a salary for each person under appointment or of listing each individual in the pension fund. Had we been consistent with our position that each person was under appointment, we would have been much more of a help in establishing identity for a number of wives.

In the mid-1960s we were challenged about institutional sexism. Most of the single people under appointment were women. The fact that single men had received the same salary as single women made no difference in the emotional climate of the day. The Commission appointed a committee to consider the concerns of women, and they spent two years working on the problem of support.

There were many different opinions among the women in the missionary/fraternal workers group. The women pressing the liberation issues insisted that a single woman receive the same pay as a married man—"equal pay for equal work." It was then that we realized how we had been trying to blend the assumptions of a support system with a salary system. The missionary wives were disenfranchised by this report. Even though they were appointed, received assignments, and played an important role in the work of the church, the committee would not agree to their receiving a salary unless it was a professional assignment, such as teaching or nursing. When COEMAR received the report, it recognized that it was incomplete and unsatisfactory. It was too late in COEMAR's life for it to deal with the remaining problems. We recognized too late that we were trying to deal with too many conflicting assumptions and pressures—equality in income, parity with pastors, and so forth. The unsolved problems were bequeathed to COEMAR's successors.

The staff salaries of the Foreign Boards had not been built on the same support system. Perhaps it was because they were living and operating in the American scene. However, these Boards and COEMAR had tried to keep their staff salaries low, and they had resisted the tendency to make big differences because of rank. They were always conscious of their missionary colleagues. On the other hand, there was always pressure to raise the General Secretary's salary in order to preserve some parity with the other agencies of the General Assembly. Members of the Commission often focused attention on that one salary, feeling that other salaries in the staff would be adjusted if they raised that one.

John Smith resisted this sort of pressure. When he was criticized by other board secretaries for making them look bad, he would insist that the level was too high for all of them. On the other hand, some staff members in COEMAR were having trouble making ends meet financially. We finally asked a staff team to work on the problem. We established the same link with the median salary for pastors as the missionary/fraternal workers system, and then established a formula that did recognize additional income for certain levels of responsibility. This system was also a system of compromises, blending equality and reward for responsibility. The proposal also permitted some allowances for children in college and for the support of aged parents. It was far from perfect, but we felt that it was much better than the competitive tension of the other system.[3]

We met resistance from Commission members who were concerned that we had eliminated merit raises and from members who were concerned that the Commission's General Secretary was the lowest paid of the general secretaries in the United Presbyterian Church. However, the Commission approved the plan, and a later survey showed that COEMAR's high-level salaries were lower than those in the other agencies, and the low-level salaries were higher. We had been working for just such a narrowing of the salary spread.

8

Participation
in Ecumenical
Organizations

Presbyterians had been active participants in the ecumenical movement from its beginning. They were to be found serving on committees and councils, and on the staffs of local, state, national, and international organizations.

Thus United Presbyterians understood the ecumenical movement as an extension of their own ministry. Generally speaking, they were able to avoid the "we/they" attitude which expresses tension between a denomination and an ecumenical organization. United Presbyterians have felt free to accept calls to staff positions in the ecumenical movement because their denomination still clearly owns them, they are still a part of their own church. The Commission tried to strengthen this feeling by holding an annual reception for the United Presbyterians who were working in the National Council.

Presbyterians feel comfortable working in most ecumenical organizations because they operate in a similar structure. We are used to attending assemblies, participating in committees, and making decisions by majority vote. Some concern was expressed that the presence of new churches from Asia, Africa, and Latin America, and the presence of the Orthodox and the Pentecostals, would change the style of the World Council and make it more difficult for Presbyterians to participate. So far that concern has been unfounded.

The Commission's position that the churches are God's instrument for mission was carried into our participation in the Division of World Mission and Evangelism of the World Council. Since that division was the former International Missionary Council made up of mission councils, not churches, COEMAR was not directly a member of that division, but John Smith was selected as a member of the divisional committee (called the Commission on World Mission and Evangelism). The Division of Foreign Missions of the National Council was a member council, and we were so active in the DFM that our staff were selected to participate in many of the international meetings.

One of the statements at the New Delhi meeting of the World Council when the Division of World Mission and Evangelism was formed was that the mission concerns of this organization were not confined to the former foreign mission areas, they were concerned with "mission on six continents." In COEMAR we interpreted this slogan to mean that the division would now be concerned with the mission and evangelism activities that took place inside the United States. Until that time the International Missionary Council contacts with the United States had been its Foreign Mission Boards. The member council from North America was the Division of Foreign Missions. The Commission took the position that the Division of Home Missions of the National Council would have as much relationship as the other division. At the first meeting of the Commission on World Mission and Evangelism, held in Mexico in 1963, the same theme of mission on six continents was emphasized. John Smith worked to have the American representative on the executive committee be the head of the Division of Home Missions. This shift was a real change for both the staff in Geneva and the home mission people in America. Neither was prepared for it, but a beginning was made.

Four of the functional service activities that we described earlier received special attention through programs that were related to the Division of World Mission and Evangelism (DWME): theological education, medical missions, Christian literature, and mass media. In each of these activities, staff members from COEMAR played an important role.

The Theological Education Fund (TEF) was the result of a survey made by the Sealantic Fund, one of the Rockefeller organizations. The survey pointed out that theological education had been neglected by mission organizations, and the Sealantic Fund offered two million dollars if the mission organizations would match it. The proposal was made in the late 1950s when church contributions were increasing, and the Presbyterian Board pledged five hundred thousand dollars. The money was raised, and the TEF was established in 1957 with four million dollars to spend in five years. It was not a crash program in the sense that it would complete a task in a short period of time; it was a "shot in the arm" program that would raise the level of theological education and count on the churches to continue the progress. John Smith commented that its cost to the Presbyterians would be far more than the five hundred thousand given to the fund, for it would create pressures for more support in the seminaries to which we were related. John served as chairman of the committee and gave excellent leadership as this program developed.

The TEF worked very well. It provided books for libraries, improved the textbook selection available, established new graduate-level seminaries, helped train leadership, and created regional associations of theological schools. Its mandate was renewed for a second period, and then the work was merged into the World Council as the Program for Theological Education.

Another special concern was medical missions. At a conference on Salvation and Healing held in Germany at Tübingen University, one of the subjects discussed was the separation of the Christian community from health concerns as mission hospitals improved their professional competence. Many mission hospitals had become so developed and so sophisticated in procedures that the churches felt no involvement in their work. The hospitals were expensive to run and spent their resources on the care of the patients who crowded their waiting rooms. This natural concentration on the curative side of medical ministry meant they were serving a smaller portion of the expanding population in the countries they had come to serve.

The mission hospitals argued that they were in themselves an expression of the Christian community, and they continued to demonstrate God's love and concern for all people through their service. However, it was true that they seldom involved the local congregation in these ministries, and the nonmedical part of the church did not feel itself a part of the healing ministry.

The Tübingen Report emphasized the healthy person as a part of a healthy community. It argued that the church has a concern for such healthy communities and that the congregations should be healing communities. The Commission had been working in the field of public health for a number of years and had already made a decision to shift more resources in that direction. Then a new emphasis appeared, closely linked to public health, called community health. It was an approach that involved more of the community in preventive activities as well as in treating simple medical problems. Hospitals and doctors were used for serious cases, clinics and paramedicals for simple needs. The idea of the clinic for simple needs had long been used in medical missions, but a new emphasis would be the training of local people to provide primary health care.

As these issues were discussed, it was felt that some international coordination of the many experiments and the many applications for financial support would be helpful. The relief agencies in Germany and Switzerland were interested in medical ministries, a natural outgrowth of their relief work. Jim McGilvray was called to the World Council staff to work on these problems, and the Christian Medical Commission was formed. It served both the Division of World Mission and Evangelism and the Division of Interchurch Aid, Refugees, and World Service.

John and Jean Sibley, medical missionaries in Korea, had been concerned that the hospital at Taegu was not serving the poor of Korea. Though they did charity work and sent mobile clinics to some villages, their treatment was still expensive and not available to all who needed it. They proposed an experiment in community health for the island of Kojedo, a few miles off the coast. With a limited geographical area and few existing medical facilities, it seemed a good spot for such an experiment. We encouraged John and Jean to go ahead with their plans, but we also knew that the experiment would cost more than COEMAR could provide. We asked the Christian Medical Commission to consider it for a project, and they agreed. Resources from Europe were secured and the project got under way. The problems that finally brought the experiment to a close were internal to Korea: community relations, government refusal to grant status to the workers, and tensions within the medical community.

Christian literature was another effort for special attention. The Division of Foreign Missions of the National Council of Churches had a Committee on World Literacy and Christian Literature (commonly called Lit-Lit). Most agencies assigned literature people to this committee, though often they were people whose main focus was on interpretation to the church in the United States. Lit-Lit thought it would benefit by having someone from general administration on its committee and I was asked to chair the committee.

About that time a World Conference on Christian Literature was called to meet in Germany. Because of some international dynamics in the situation, it was felt that an American should preside, so I was asked.

The European penchant for separate mission societies had extended to the specialized fields, and the literature societies were separate mission organizations with printing presses and bookstores through Asia, Africa, and the Middle East. They were members of the mission councils, but they were a law unto themselves in how they went about their work. Lit-Lit, on the other hand, provided expertise and coordination for programs that were run by the member agencies or by the councils of churches in the various countries.

As the conference progressed, the participants saw the need for special efforts in Christian literature production and distribution that could be coordinated on an international basis. The thinking was influenced by the Theological Education Fund which was just getting under way. The idea of extra resources to strengthen existing publishing efforts and to conduct experiments was very attractive. It was not easy to sell the idea of another fund to the leaders of the Division of World Mission and Evangelism or of the mission agencies. People wanted more experience with the fund idea before they started too many others. However, the Christian Literature Fund (CLF) was finally approved as a related agency of the DWME.

One of the most significant contributions made by the CLF was the creation of an understanding of the publishing function among the churches that had inherited printing presses and bookstores from the Missions. The need for a sound business operation that planned its projects from the selection of the writers through a good distribution system was evident in almost every country. The CLF provided as much through its consultation and training of the people responsible for the work as it did in actual grants.

Broadcasting was another area of rapid development that received special attention. Burton Martin had been on the staff of the Presbyterian Board with responsibilities in the Interpretation Department. Filmstrips and motion pictures were prepared for the American churches to help them understand this aspect of our outreach. He also provided advice and equipment for missionaries who were using such aids in their work.

In 1948 Burt had been instrumental in forming a cooperative group of foreign mission agencies for working on these activities. It was called the Radio, Visual Education and Mass Communications Committee (RAVEMCCO). For a time he carried the staff work for this committee. When the National Council of Churches was formed in 1950, this organization became one of the program departments of the Division of Foreign Missions and eventually grew to have its own staff.

Burt was also instrumental in forming the World Association of Christian Broadcasters (WACB), a group that brought together people involved in religious broadcasting. In Europe, and in many countries that had been colonies of the European powers, the government broadcasting systems had departments of religious broadcasting that worked with the churches. The staff members of these departments wanted an association where they could exchange information and ideas. In addition to such government activities, there were a number of church-owned broadcasting stations that had been started by mission organizations. They were usually cooperative projects supported by several organizations, and those who worked in them also became members of the world association.

As broadcasting technology improved, these church-owned projects grew, and soon they were seeking resources from agencies in more than one country, often competing for support. A Coordinating Committee for Christian Broadcasting (CCCB) was formed under the Division of World Mission and Evangelism, and it became the place where contributions by mission agencies to these major broadcasting centers were negotiated. Two groups were involved in church-related broadcasting—CCCB and WACB. They often involved some of the same persons. It was inevitable that the merger of these two groups would be considered. They merged into the World Association of Christian Communication and assumed the work of the Christian Literature Fund.

These activities show that COEMAR was quite involved in trying to deal with mission concerns from a world perspective. At the same time, many were asking about the place of the confessional bodies in relation to the ecumenical movement. The World Presbyterian Alliance and the

Lutheran World Federation had member churches that felt at home in the confessional family but would not join the World Council of Churches. However, the members of these confessional bodies faced problems when they entered church unions across confessional lines. The united churches, such as those in Japan, the Philippines, and South India inherited membership in as many as four confessional organizations.

Other problems arose when some of the confessional bodies became instruments of mission program. The Lutheran World Federation is the most obvious example, providing a channel for relief programs, mission activity, and other cooperative ventures for the Lutheran family. We faced such problems related to the Radio Voice of the Gospel, the shortwave radio station in Ethiopia. For a number of years an interdenominational group had been trying to get permission to build a shortwave station in Addis Ababa. Such a transmitter could reach most of Africa, the Middle East, and southern Asia. While these negotiations continued, the Lutherans used a direct contact with the emperor and secured the permit in the name of the Lutheran World Federation. The interdenominational group was then invited to join the project, but clearly as a junior partner. It was a disillusioning experience from an ecumenical viewpoint.

There are two main approaches to ecumenical activity. The Lutherans in this project communicated the idea that they felt the way to be a good Christian is to be a good Lutheran. As a Presbyterian I had been conditioned to the approach that the way to be a good Presbyterian is to be a good Christian. The result of the first attitude is that the group cooperates only when the work cannot be done alone; we in COEMAR tried to hold to the second approach— that we should do alone only what we cannot do cooperatively. When suggestions were made that the World Presbyterian Alliance might begin mission program activities, we resisted the idea and said our program support would go through the World Council of Churches.

During the 1950s and 1960s another development had helped form our position. In the mid-1950s the Presbyterian Board had called a meeting in Hong Kong of representatives of five of the churches with which it was related in mission. The topic was how these churches could begin to work together in mission. A follow-up meeting the next

year organized the Asia Council on Ecumenical Mission.
There was no church group in Asia through which these
churches might meet together. It was the beginning of
regionalism in the ecumenical movement.

The existence of this group was quite disturbing to the
World Council of Churches (wcc) and the International
Missionary Council (imc). Regional organizations might
become a barrier between the member churches or the
member councils and the world organizations. They were
unhappy to see the Presbyterians going off on their own.
Although the Presbyterians called the first meeting, it was
the churches in Asia, many of them united churches and
related to several mission agencies, that had established
the Asia Council on Ecumenical Mission. After a very tense
meeting in Bangkok in 1956, which started out to discredit
the Asia Council on Ecumenical Mission, the representatives of the wcc and imc admitted they had been wrong. A
much broader meeting was called for Prapat, Indonesia,
the next year. The East Asia Christian Conference was
organized, and the Asia Council on Ecumenical Mission
went out of existence. This experience influenced coemar's
response to still another approach to international cooperation in mission.

During the 1960s the Paris Mission Society was integrat-
ing its overseas Missions into the churches that had grown
out of their work. To be on equal footing with other
churches, the Paris Mission Society had to be recognized
as the official overseas mission arm of the Reformed
Churches in France and Switzerland. Then these churches
formed an organization known as ceva (Communauté
Évangélique d'Action Apostolique), in which they together
distribute the mission resources the churches contribute.
Since that time a similar organization, known as the Council on World Mission, has been formed by churches related
to the mission work of the United Reformed Church of
England and Wales.

The Commission examined this approach and pulled
away from it. We had tried a similar move with some of
our related churches in the Asia Council on Ecumenical
Mission and it had merged with the ecumenical movement.
Furthermore, this approach seemed to institutionalize missionary history. The only common bond of these churches
was their tie to a particular mission organization in the
West, and we were trying to break out of that history. We

were trying to set both the churches and ourselves free to be full members of the ecumenical movement.

Since we had, in a sense, thrown our lot with the ecumenical movement, we pressed the DWME of the World Council to take a more active role in coordinating mission activities in those countries where more than one nationality was involved with the churches. Their Joint Action for Mission emphasis in the early days seemed to be moving them in this direction, and programs such as the TEF were helping in specialized fields. However, they still carried their International Missionary Council history, and that organization had not been a program group.

One new possibility, mentioned in chapter 7, was the exchanging of mission personnel among the churches. The Asia Council on Ecumenical Mission had had this matter high on its agenda, and its successor, the East Asia Christian Conference, had such a program. Two hundred mission personnel were exchanged among Asian churches in the 1960s. The idea of working on this program from a world perspective was approved at the 1961 assembly of the Division of World Mission and Evangelism, and we in COEMAR pressed the staff to implement it. I was invited to read a paper on the subject at the next meeting of the DWME Executive Committee. Don Smith and I prepared the paper based on COEMAR's experience in trying to implement "three-way mission" and on a conference on the matter that Don had attended in Asia. We pointed out some of the problems we had run into as a single agency, problems that would be resolved by an ecumenical approach.

There was quite a reaction from several European representatives against the idea, claiming that it would make the WCC into a supermission society. There was a positive response from the representatives of the Division of Inter-Church Aid who were at the meeting, for they had been recruiting and sponsoring ecumenical teams for years. The result of the discussion was an interdivision committee on the Ecumenical Sharing of Personnel. Unfortunately this committee did not get far with its assignment before it became a sounding board for the idea of a moratorium on the sending of missionaries. That idea will be discussed in chapter 10. The idea of the Ecumenical Sharing of Personnel was eventually included in a broader study on the Ecumenical Sharing of Resources.

Another occasion when COEMAR tried to get the World

Council involved in a new approach was in the follow-up of the Six-Day War between Egypt and Israel. This war created an internal crisis in Egypt and Lebanon, and all American personnel were evacuated. Some of the fraternal workers came to the States, but most of them went to other spots in the Mediterranean area until it seemed safe to return to their posts.

This crisis seemed to present an opportunity to examine our relations with the churches in those countries, especially the number of personnel we should be sending to them. The fraternal workers from Lebanon did not keep in close touch with us, and many returned to their posts as soon as government restrictions were lifted. Egypt was slower to reopen its doors to Americans, so we had a chance to discuss with the fraternal workers what we were proposing.

It was our feeling that being tied to an American church was a liability for the Evangelical Church in Egypt (known as the Synod of the Nile), that the presence of the American fraternal workers might prove an embarrassment to them. They would have to function for several weeks without the Americans anyway, so why not give them time to think through their program and decide what personnel they needed. This sort of examination would be easier while the fraternal workers were not present. We suggested that no one return for a year, during which they would be given temporary assignments elsewhere. We also suggested that the conversation about future needs be conducted by the DWME of the World Council so there would be more freedom to consider the use of personnel from other countries.

Meanwhile, back in Egypt the Synod of the Nile was taking a different approach. It wanted to show loyalty to Egypt and to its friends in America, and it was trying to show the government that not everyone in America was pro-Israel. When we sent the synod five thousand dollars relief money to help families who may have suffered loss in the war, the synod turned the sum over to the Red Crescent as a gift from its friends in America. The synod personnel were not enthusiastic about having the World Council come to discuss the future with them, and they refused to participate in those discussions unless we were there. They welcomed the chance to think through what personnel they might want from the United Presbyterian Church, but they accepted with reluctance the proposal that they might get teachers from churches in some other nation, such as India. The government killed that idea by refusing to grant visas for such personnel. It was an interesting experiment, new to the staff of the World Council, new to the churches involved. It did point up the fact that bringing change in some of the mission situations would require more from the ecumenical organizations than holding conferences and publishing papers.

Most of this chapter has been devoted to our activities in the DWME and its related organizations. We were still following our mission history. However, United Presbyterians were also quite involved with other aspects of the World Council's life.

We have already described the beginnings of Inter-Church Aid during World War II and how it grew as natural disasters and political emergencies created more refugees and required a response from the churches. As the Division of Inter-Church Aid, Refugees, and World Service (DICARWS), it coordinated a great number of programs and was the channel for large financial resources. Its coordination of relief work was excellent. The leaders experimented with ecumenical teams in special service projects, and they instituted a project system that provided a channel of interchurch aid for many different activities. They explored development programs as they shifted from crisis relief to long-term reconstruction in certain situations.

The early leaders of that division were from Europe, and they brought with them some caricatures of the missionary movement which hindered their perceptions. My first impression of DICARWS was that it was so antimissionary that it could not realize it was repeating the mistakes of that era. In some discussions I felt that the leaders hoped the mission agencies would make no changes, for that would destroy their caricatures and prejudices. They were sure the wave of the future was interchurch aid.

Eugene Blake was chairperson of this committee in the early 1960s. He did much to bring a more responsible involvement of the churches from Asia and Africa in the division's work. The division was criticized as being a "donors' club" made up of relief people, as paternalistic in their way as the mission had ever been. Gene worked for changes to break that image.

The involvement of COEMAR with this division came through the denomination's relief efforts. In our church a special committee related to the General Council supervised the use of money raised through the One Great Hour of Sharing. This offering had originally been a coordinated effort of all major denominations, promoted in the secular mass media, and gaining a good response. Funds from the United Presbyterian share that were spent outside the United States had been channeled through the Board of Foreign Missions, and COEMAR inherited the task.

As there had been coordination in raising the money, there was also coordination in responding to crises. The American instrument for this coordination was Church World Service, and similar national coordinating organizations existed in Europe. It was the work of these agencies that DICARWS coordinated on the world scene.

Church World Service was an effective relief organization, and when it was meeting crises such as floods or earthquakes, there was little conflict with the mission agencies. But when it became involved in long-range reconstruction programs, or when it attempted to deal with what was called "endemic need," it was often dealing with the same church leaders in other countries that the mission agencies were working with. It became evident that Church World Service and the Division of Foreign Missions of the National Council of Churches were developing a number of overlapping interests. However, both organizations were supported by the same churches, though some of the denominations had separate relief agencies. After several years of separate existence, Church World Service and the Division of Foreign Missions merged to become the Division of Overseas Ministries of the National Council.

Dan Pattison, the treasurer, had carried the relief responsibilities for COEMAR and he became our major contact with Church World Service. Through this responsibility he also became involved with the Division of Inter-Church Aid, Refugees, and World Service of the World Council. He was a good participant in such discussions. He kept the various staff members informed of issues, consulted with them about budget matters, and was sensitive to the human concerns in disaster situations. However, he was the treasurer, and we felt that more attention needed to be given to the relief concerns than he could give with his other responsibilities. In the late 1960s we established a special office to deal with all the concerns of relief and rehabilitation with a full-time staff member.

John Smith played a prominent role in two other developments in the World Council—the Program to Combat Racism and the Commission of the Churches on the Development of Peoples. We will be describing these events in chapter 9.

The Commission was concerned that all the churches have their chance to participate in the ecumenical movement. We contributed to the travel pool for council assemblies and made special grants to see that women and youth could be present. Shortly after Gene Blake became General Secretary I commented to him that the committee meetings I had attended were still loaded with Western church leaders. He explained that the World Council still depended on the member churches to pay the travel expenses of many committee members, and it was the Western churches that could afford that expense. He proposed that some of us provide money for a travel pool for the committees, not just the assembly. I carried the proposal to COEMAR with the recommendation that we make $250,000 available which could be spent over a ten-year period. Then the churches could take another look at the problem. The Commission supported the idea, and the World Council used the grant to approach other agencies. The Methodists promised $100,000 to be paid over the ten-year period. The plan had its effect. The finance officer of the World Council commented that the Uppsala Assembly was the first time he had not had to caution the nominating committee about the financial effects of its proposals for membership on the Central Committee and the Executive Committee.

The number of Westerners on these committees was reduced, and that situation presented the United Presbyterians with a problem at the Uppsala Assembly. It was the mid-1960s, and American churches were concerned about minority representation in all their activities. When the nominating committee reported, the U.S. delegation to the Central Committee had only one Black, and that person was from one of the black churches. Only the United Presbyterians, the United Church of Christ, and the Methodists had enough flexibility in their delegations to make a change. The United Church of Christ made a change and the Methodists were prepared to make another. The United Presbyterian delegation was the problem. John Smith was a delegate because he was nominated as a president, Bill Thompson was a delegate because the Stated Clerk has some ecumenical responsibilities, and Jim McCord was a delegate because he was the chair of the Faith and Order Commission. Jim McCord withdrew and Edler Hawkins, a former Moderator of our General Assembly, was named in his place. This switch was made after considerable discussion about whether Jim McCord or Bill Thompson would be the one to withdraw. The 1960s caught us unprepared for many of the steps we had to take, steps we needed to take if we were to repair some of the mistakes of our past. A new focus for mission was emerging, and it would have an effect on all our activities.

9

A New Focus
for Mission

The social upheaval of the 1960s forced churches to reexamine their programs and their practices. A new focus for mission was emerging. For over a century the church had defined mission in geographical terms: the "foreign" mission agency worked outside the country, the "home" mission agency worked within the nation. In the 1960s we realized that mission was no longer defined geographically—there was one mission of the church to all people; the mission of the church exists on six continents.

Mission was still concerned with people, but it was seen in the way people were affected by issues such as justice, liberation, racism, sexism, economic oppression, and human rights. In the light of these issues the church responded to various situations. These issues shaped our activities in other nations and forced us to examine how our nation's actions affected people in other parts of the world.

In the mid-1950s we sensed the beginning of an anti-institutional attitude. It was felt that the churches' concern for survival would undercut the motive for mission. We had concentrated so much on self-government and self-support that the churches were preoccupied with internal affairs. My description of the structural change that occupied so much of COEMAR's time and energy would support such a criticism. However, these efforts were accompanied by a concern for God's mission to the world, and the changes in relationships were made so that the churches could get on with their part of that mission. One of the emphases at the Lake Mohonk Consultation in the mid-1950s was "evangelism beyond the church." In student circles there was emphasis on the life and mission of the church and discussion about the new frontiers of mission.

Theological writings in support of these emphases spoke

of "going outside the camp" to reach people who had no knowledge of God's reconciliation of the world through Christ. Our mission activity should take place where we could perceive Christ's redemptive activity at work, and his redemptive activity would be seen at those places where people were struggling to be fully human. Thus if people are struggling for human dignity in a voter registration drive, then the church should be with them in that struggle. Christian missionaries should be out in the world where they could make a greater impact on issues that directly affect people's lives.

Such thinking led several clergy to leave the pastorate for secular activities, and the church had to decide whether such positions qualified for continuing their status as clergy. The Commission made some assignments to secular posts in other countries. The Laymen Abroad program was given special emphasis, and we experimented with a ministry to international civil servants.[1]

Masao Takenaka of Japan gave an illustration that we used often. "Christians have been 'fishers of men' in a muddy river called the world. When they catch one, they place him in a clean pool called the church. However, a person does not really live in that clean pool, he goes back into the muddy river for his everyday existence. The church should recognize the muddy river as the place where its people witness." It is true that in many of the mission fields the Christian community had to become a separate community, a "clean pool," to shelter converts from the pressures of a hostile society. It was also true that the rapid social change in the world was making such communities difficult to maintain, and the new insights into the mission of the church made their dispersal into the secular world an important strategy.

One of the problems with such strategy, however, was that we never clarified what we expected to happen in that muddy stream. We assumed that Christians would bring changes that would make life more tolerable for the poor and the oppressed; we were to be change agents for good. We no doubt were too optimistic about the effect that such efforts would have on the social structures, and within a decade frustration and discouragement set in among those people who, with high hopes, had gone into the secular arena to work for social justice.

Iran was the country where COEMAR tried the most experiments in work with secular agencies. The Evangelical Church was small and could not absorb all the institutions the Mission had started. Some of the fraternal workers were related to the church, and some were working in institutions that were not directly under church control.

Medical work in Iran went through a rapid transformation in a little over a decade. The Mission had pioneered in medical services and established hospitals in many of the larger communities. The modernization of Iran moved at a rapid pace after World War II, and by the late 1950s well-equipped and modern government institutions overshadowed the Mission hospitals. The latter had neither the facilities nor the specialists to provide many of the services people expected. Mission hospitals were unable to attract paying patients, and COEMAR could not provide all the subsidies needed. The medical work was consolidated, and a service that once had ten hospitals and clinics was reduced to three hospitals and a well-baby clinic. These four centers were eventually reduced to two, and the plan was to upgrade the hospital in Tabrīz to a top-level medical center. We appointed a thoracic surgeon as a step in upgrading that hospital, but he soon discovered that we could not afford his specialty. If he operated twice a week, it would tie up the operating room and laboratory facilities so that regular surgery could not take place. We had neither the facilities nor the financial strength for that sort of development.

Contacts with the medical schools in both Meshed and Tabrīz opened new possibilities. The hospital in Meshed worked out a contract for becoming a teaching hospital for the medical school, and the hospital in Tabrīz became the nurses training center for the university. Each opportunity seemed to be a breakthrough in working with the government in a Muslim country; both turned out to be disappointments. The Iranian political scene was in constant flux, and university administrators had little continuity in their assignments. The government people who signed the contracts were not on the scene long enough to see to their fulfillment, and their successors often showed little interest. The mission personnel who were working with the government universities found themselves caught in internal political tensions. Neither arrangement lasted very long.

One of the programs begun by the Mission had been a community service center in a poor section of Teheran, and from this base a contact was made with the Ministry of Social Services. A trained social worker was appointed to Iran and worked with the government ministry as a consultant. He made several contributions, but also found that working with a government ministry was an adventure in frustration.

The education experiments centered around two institutions. The Community School had started as a school for missionary children, but it had accepted students from other groups. In the 1960s the American Community in Iran rapidly increased. At one time there were more than six thousand Americans in Teheran. The Community School was bulging at the seams, yet there was no one to assume responsibility for its program except the person we appointed as principal. The school needed more local involvement and control. The strategy we followed was to organize a board that would agree to assume responsibility for the school. We were participants in the board, and we contributed the property. However, we no longer made missionary appointments to the faculty. We were willing to recruit teachers, but they would have to be paid by the school.

The other situation was the Iran-Bethel School. It had been started by a fraternal worker gathering some Iranian girls who had finished their formal education but who were unable to go to work or to further schooling. It started in a residence and expanded into the neighboring buildings. The school ran a social service center where the girls learned some social responsibility. Girls kept returning and new ones appeared until the classes included the second year of college. It became a junior college whose facilities were inadequate and whose academic level was low.

The Commission organized a team of educators to go to Teheran to study the situation. The team found that the school could not continue as it was, nor would the alumni and the community stand for our closing it. They recommended that a college be organized in Teheran, established under Iranian law and controlled by an Iranian board on which Christian communities would be represented along with other Iranian groups. The assets of Iran-Bethel School, which were few, and some money that COEMAR held for education in Iran would be our contribution. With much hard work and many creative initiatives by two women fraternal workers, Damavand College developed into the outstanding women's school in Iran. It was a liberating influence on Iranian women until the Khomeni revolution.

Other experiments were attempted, but did not have much success. Working with secular institutions to accomplish the goals of the Christian mission is not easy. Within ten years, support for this approach was receding. Political perceptions and theological positions shifted. The world was no longer good, the work of a benevolent creator, and the arena for Christ's redemptive activity; it was the abode of the "principalities and powers." The political, social, and economic systems of this world were regarded as basically demonic. The only hope was to contend against these established structures and to help a new and just order emerge. We discovered institutional racism and sexism, and we realized that the church was an instrument of oppression along with other institutions.

The first wave of anti-institutionalism had perceived the church as concerned with survival; the second period saw the church and its institutions as inflexible, designed to serve in a past era, so captured by the disciplines of their professionalism that they could no longer be instruments of change. On the other hand, some people saw the need for an institutional base if programs to help the poor and oppressed were to exist. Church buildings were pressed into community service. Head start programs, tutoring services, health clinics, food banks, and many other services appeared in these buildings which had often been closed during the week. When community organizations wanted to put pressure into the political system, they tried to get support from the churches. One of the divisive issues of those days was whether the church as a corporate body should take a stand on sensitive issues or whether this was the role of individuals in the society. The Commission felt that the corporate body should take a stand, and many of its activities were pointed in that direction.

As we moved through the turmoil of that decade, COEMAR maintained the position expressed in its purpose that the church's task in every situation was to make Jesus Christ known, to demonstrate God's concern by entering into the sufferings of people, and to call people to be his disciples. Many voices in the church, and some within our staff, felt that it was a waste of time to try to reach individuals with the gospel message. The important task was to change the oppressive situations in which people lived. However, the concern for reaching people with the good news was never dropped from our programs and priorities. In 1968 we established the Office of Evangelism and Church Development, and made many efforts to keep the evangelism and social action emphases combined.

Our efforts to shift to a new focus in mission were through program emphases. Some of them are described in the sections that follow.

FRONTIER INTERNS

The Frontier Intern program was designed by Margaret Flory, Secretary for Student World Relations, as a follow-up of the 1960 Student Volunteer Quadrennial in Athens, Ohio. The theme had dealt with the frontiers of mission, and Margaret wanted some of the outstanding students to have an experience in mission as they were shaping their careers. The experience was to be a combination of study and work on one of the emerging frontiers: racial tensions, university world, resurgent religions, developing nationalism, and others. Even at this time the term "frontier" had lost its geographical dimension. The assignment would be to explore a new sociological frontier where Christian witness was absent or inadequate.

Like all new ideas, this one had rough going. It was different from the regular short-term assignment in that it must be to explore something new. We did not appoint frontier interns to fill established jobs. The interns were to live on a subsistence income, were to work under an experienced counselor, and were to have a study aspect to their project. The idea that young, inexperienced personnel could really break new ground was not easy to accept, and a new program that requires changes in established personnel procedures is seldom welcome. However, we persisted, and the program was established.

There were some good results. Many of the assignments in the early days of the program were on the frontier of the university world, and it was in this area that some of the happiest experiences occurred. The experience was determinative for some people as they shaped their careers, and several of them have continued to play important roles in relation to southern Africa.

Of course there were problems. We assigned some interns to projects in countries where we had few connections, so there were problems with financial transfers and with giving them support when they were in difficulty. Sometimes local arrangements were not clear; sometimes the local counselors were transferred from the scene. In spite of our careful recruiting, sometimes an intern was not the right person for the situation. The intern program was for people who can live with freedom and with the uncertainty of the unstructured, and many people cannot tell how they will react to such a situation until they are in it.

We learned through this experience that the new wine of a fresh idea cannot be poured into the receptacle of an established structure. If we had designed the program and assigned it to the mission personnel staff in COEMAR, we would not have seen any interns. The staff who would have carried responsibility did not grasp the concept and had little interest in dealing with it.

We attempted to develop the program in an ecumenical setting, but only the Methodists and the United Church of Christ showed much interest, and the only financing available in the early days was from COEMAR. The Methodists and the United Church of Christ did participate later and became a part of the supervising committee. Margaret Flory was the administrator, and I chaired the committee that worked with her. The staff members who became a part of that committee did support the idea, and thus support in the staff was strengthened. Margaret was creative in ideas, a tireless worker, always assuming more responsibilities than she could handle easily. She had a great ability to draw numbers of people into a project so they could make a contribution, and many of COEMAR's programs were enriched through the contacts made by her.

The program was administered out of COEMAR's offices for ten years. The focus of the program shifted with the mood of the people involved. The first interns were concerned about the churches with which they worked, but a later group felt that those churches were irrelevant, that what counted was the way American power was being misused in other nations.

The Frontier Intern program had an ambivalent, love-suspicion relationship with the Commission. It insisted on the freedom to "do its own thing," would not use the ecumenical center at Stony Point for orientation, developed its own projects apart from staff procedures, and then complained because the Commission did not reshape its activity along the lines of the Frontier Intern program. The interns appreciated the fact that COEMAR would have such a program, but many of them treated us as a church bureaucracy that could not be trusted.

The Commission did learn from the Frontier Intern program. Many of the changes in personnel practice and the attempts to get more flexibility into the appointment list grew out of experiences of the interns. Some of the program assignments developed into longer-term activities, and some of the difficulties, such as those faced by the couple trying to contact international civil servants, warned us away from some superficial approaches in program. Some of the interns who served in southern Africa were a great influence in our approach to that area.

As the program developed, it drew attention from many areas, and recruits began to appear from other nations. It showed signs of developing into an international program, and we saw that a truly international program could not be funded entirely by Americans and administered from New York. We entered long negotiations with other churches, with the World Student Christian Federation, and with the WCC Division of World Mission and Evangelism. Out of these negotiations came an arrangement for the program to be directed, supported, and administered by an international group. This experiment has developed well and is still having its effect.

EMERGING ECONOMIES

During the process of transferring administrative responsibility to churches and institutions, we realized that we were managing some endowments for some of these former mission schools and hospitals. These investments should have been transferred to them for investment in their own countries. In that way the institution could strengthen the local economy. We were aware of problems caused by entrepreneurs in many developing nations who kept all their money in European or American banks, thus further weakening the economy out of which they were making their fortunes.

These discussions were being held during the first United

Nations Development Decade when great stress was being placed on Europe and North America helping the new nations of Asia and Africa, the rich nations helping the poor nations, in order to develop their economies along the patterns of the West. America had a large foreign aid program and encouraged private investment abroad. There was a sense in which COEMAR was already investing abroad, for it owned stock in American corporations that were at work in other nations. However, we were aware that this type of investment was not always beneficial to the foreign nation—the high rate of return moved the wealth back to the United States. The multinational corporations were just beginning to appear on the international scene.

In one of our staff discussions, it was proposed that COEMAR make its own investments in other countries. We were concerned about the economic situation in those countries. We knew from the impact of "the green revolution" in southern Asia that something that raised the economic level of the entire community would help the church. If we could show that such investments were sound and brought some return to the investor, then we might persuade the United Presbyterian Foundation and the Pension Fund to put part of their funds into such ventures. It was the difference between investing endowment funds and spending program funds. At that time a million dollars invested in Wall Street would return fifty thousand dollars for program. If we were willing to settle for a smaller rate of return, that million invested in an emerging economy might bring twenty thousand dollars in program money. We would have thirty thousand dollars less to spend in a particular country, but we would have put a million dollars to work in that country. And if the investment provided jobs for people and was in a firm that had good social goals, we would have achieved part of our purpose as a church in mission. It was an attempt to use investments as an instrument of mission.

The chairperson of COEMAR's Finance Committee reminded us that we were making a departure from present practices. The Finance Committee had three guidelines in supervising our investments: protect the capital, make the capital grow to match inflation, and produce income for program. The only restrictions they had concerned investments in the alcohol or tobacco industries; they had inherited these restrictions from the Boards of Foreign Missions.

If the capital became an instrument for accomplishing the church's social and mission goals, then the new guideline might affect the results in one of the other three.

It was in this area of responsibility that we confronted what is known as the "prudent man" rule. Members of an organization such as COEMAR are trustees of the endowments and responsible before the law for fulfilling the first three guidelines of our Finance Committee, and they were expected to be prudent in that management. Any decision that deliberately endangered capital or accepted lower income than was generally available was culpable. Therefore our experiments had to be with unrestricted reserves, funds that could be spent as well as invested. We set aside a million dollars for such exploration.

We launched the effort with enthusiasm, caution, and some disappointment. The church had never made money through its mission activity, and any return on profits should be spent in the country in which the investment was made. We knew that other agencies in "475" were considering the same program, so we tried to make the venture interdenominational. However, each treasurer had an idea he thought was the right one, and none of us was willing to adjust our ideas enough to work together, so we all went our separate ways.

Since this venture was an investment in the economy of the other nations, we decided to keep it separate from our regular staff processes and to work outside church channels overseas. We felt that the chances of confusion and misunderstanding were too great. Our hope was to participate in a separate company where we would be stockholders along with other people, but this company would have social goals compatible with the church's mission. Therefore, we formed the Emerging Economies Corporation (EEC). A few individuals bought stock, but the major stockholder was COEMAR.

The EEC never fulfilled our hopes. We were not able to prove that such a channel would protect the capital and make a return of some money for program, and we were not able to attract other investors.

While we were starting this experiment, we pressed the World Council of Churches to attempt the same effort on an international basis. They had an organization known as the Ecumenical Church Loan Fund which helped finance church buildings, and they did some exploration of working outside church channels. The report of the wcc Assembly at Uppsala, Sweden, included the suggestion, and several years later Ecumenical Development Cooperative Society (EDCS) was launched as a separate corporation. This venture was successful in its early efforts and received good support from the United Presbyterian Church.

While COEMAR was trying to make its investment funds available to emerging economies in other parts of the world, a similar discussion about the use of church investments was under way in the domestic scene. This effort was linked to our involvement in racial issues, which leads into our next subject.

ECONOMICS AND RACIAL JUSTICE

The minority communities in the United States had been bypassed in the economic development of society. When they attempted to start their own businesses, the rules of the banking community made it almost impossible for them to qualify for loans. During the 1960s there were several efforts to make loans available to these people, and the churches sponsored some of those programs.

The Presbyterian Economic Development Corporation (PEDCO) was funded with several million dollars from the reserves of the agencies. The Commission's contribution was two million dollars. The original idea was that these funds were to be seen as investment, and many of us hoped that PEDCO would show that making such loans was financially sound, that it would pay a return on the original investment and open the way for more funds to be made available. However, the leaders of PEDCO chose to treat the original investments as donations. They maintained that making low-interest loans in high-risk situations precludes any return. The General Assembly finally accepted that position, but also told them to expect no more investment from the church. Some good work has been done by PEDCO, and a number of business ventures in the minority communities have been helped.

In the EEC experiment and in PEDCO the church lost opportunities for more church funds to be invested in ways that would help them accomplish some of their mission goals. The World Council's work through EDCS may keep the possibility open, but our record as a denomination has not been encouraging.

The church also began to raise questions about its regular investments and about the social performance of the companies in which it was a stockholder. The churches were not alone in their concern; many universities and foundations also raised questions about the social responsibility of corporations. This emphasis caught the corporations off balance. Often they did not have information at hand to answer the questions posed. Annual meetings became times of challenging management about hiring practices and other issues that had not been a part of their performance review.

The Commission became involved in the Eastman Kodak problems because we owned stock. We worked closely with the Board of National Missions which had helped the presbytery in Rochester, New York, fund a community organization called Freedom, Integration, God, Honor—Today (FIGHT). One of its goals was to get more Blacks into the Eastman work force. There were a number of United Presbyterian congregations in Rochester, and not all the members were in sympathy with the community organization and the strategy of confrontation used at the Kodak annual meeting in 1967.

The community organization was known by the acronym FIGHT and was led by Rev. Franklin D. R. Florence. He had been trained well in interrupting the chairman, causing turmoil, and walking out of the meeting. A number of churches were prepared to make statements or ask questions, but the meeting was clearly in support of the management.

The experience helped me see the problems the minorities were having with the white liberals. Kodak was a liberal company; it had a good record of hiring minorities but within their own guidelines. The white liberals, and I was among them, had been setting the terms for minority participation in society. We had been willing to help minorities as long as they fit into the social structure we had established. I could see myself in that Kodak management team.

I wrote my experience at this meeting in an article called "Focus on the White Liberal." The Board of National Missions staff printed it and distributed more than thirty thousand copies.[2] It evidently spoke to the experience of many United Presbyterians.

The Commission's next involvement with this approach

was in relation to South Africa. The United Presbyterian Church had not been involved in that area of Africa through mission effort, and it was through our racial concerns that we began to pay attention to some of its issues. Some of the Frontier Intern assignments had been in southern Africa, and these contacts did much to sensitize us to the issues. A task force on southern Africa was appointed, and it brought the concerns of Church and Race, Church and Society, and Ecumenical Relations together.

We developed two lines of activity related to economic concerns. One was a series of dialogues with a consortium of banks that extended credit to the South Africa government. We challenged them on their support of a government that openly practiced apartheid. The dialogue was stimulating and may have helped the bank officials to see the social issues, but it was not effective in stopping the financial actions. Protest actions such as shifting bank accounts were important as symbols but not effective in making change.

The other line of activity was to file stockholder resolutions with companies doing business there. This approach brought us into contact with a number of corporations, but our most difficult series of discussions were with Gulf Oil. Major stockholders in Gulf Oil were a number of Presbyterian families in the Pittsburgh area where their head offices were located. When we confronted Gulf we were raising the tension level in a number of congregations.

Gulf Oil was the main oil producer in Cabinda, a Portuguese enclave in Angola. It was aligned with colonial powers in a time when strong liberation movements were trying to set Angola free. Our natural sympathies in COEMAR were with the people who were trying to rid Africa of colonialism. In African thinking, the white governments in southern Africa were really colonial remains, even though they are not colonies as such.

A coalition of various student groups and other organizations sympathetic to the Africans in that area attacked Gulf Oil for its policies, instituted boycott efforts, and planned to demonstrate at the annual meeting in 1969. John Smith went to that meeting accompanied by Don Register, a young black pastor who was a member of COEMAR. When John saw the style of disruption being used by the coalition, he refused to participate, but he gave the chairman a copy of his planned statement.

The Gulf story was far from over. There was to be another approach to the Gulf annual meeting in 1970, but the church groups were cooperating to avoid the turmoil of the year before. Their strategy was to propose a slate of directors to run against the management nominees. They planned to appoint a responsible group of people. John Smith, who had recently retired, was among them. We held twelve thousand shares of Gulf stock, and the task force asked us for proxies so they could vote all United Presbyterian shares as a block. The Executive Committee decided to keep the vote in COEMAR hands.

At the Gulf meeting the alternate slate was not the one the church groups planned, and it included Dr. Neto, a Marxist leader from West Africa, and Dr. Angela Davis, a university professor who was under indictment for having assisted a prison break in California and who had become a symbol of the white establishment's persecution of radical black leaders. The United Presbyterian Church was already in turmoil because the Council on Church and Race had made a contribution toward her defense. It was evident that this slate was a protest against Gulf management. The Commission's votes were cast for the alternate slate.

This information was given to James Kilpatrick, a conservative journalist whose syndicated column appeared in many papers across the country. He wrote about the grant to Angela Davis' defense, but the new item was the word about COEMAR votes at the Gulf meeting.

Monday morning after the column appeared the phone was busy with calls from all over the country—the power of the press. Synod and presbytery executives, already under fire over the Angela Davis matter, were far more understanding than I think I would have been. We put material giving the background of our discussions with Gulf in the mail to them that day, but we were busy for months trying to explain that our representative was casting COEMAR's vote as a protest against an insensitive management. In spite of all our explanations, the church at large felt we were one or more of the following: devious, inept, or naive. Few people agreed that casting votes for corporation directors was a proper way to make a protest.

As we dealt with these social issues we were concerned with how well the church expresses its ideals within its own life. On the matter of hiring minorities we did not do very well. The Council on Church and Race asked one of its members to study the employment records of the General Assembly agencies. There were a number of Blacks in our offices, and we assumed we had a good record. The study showed us that we had no Blacks in executive positions since Frank Wilson had retired. Some of our staff then became defensive about the difficulty of recruiting people; others mouthed the usual platitudes about wanting to get the best person regardless of race. It was pointed out that our system of recruiting staff was the "old boy network": we approached people we knew. It was startling to hear that all the black pastors in the denomination had been surveyed and that very few of them had ever been approached about a staff position. From that point on we did not fill any staff position until a minority person had been considered for the job, and I actively searched for minority candidates each time there was a vacancy that I was responsible for filling. I was not very successful, but it was a step toward an affirmative action program.

It was evident that the approach of the white community to social change was too slow. Martin Luther King had started a movement that galvanized the black community to action and in which white liberals could join. We still had visions of an integrated society run on white terms. Many of us were challenging the churches to become more integrated and bemoaning the fact that eleven o'clock on Sunday morning was the most segregated hour in American life. Most of our Church and Race activity was with this mind-set.

The Black Power movement was difficult for many of us to comprehend. It was a demand for us to accept Blacks on their terms, and not as people who would act in ways acceptable to the white community. The efforts to integrate churches gave way to efforts to strengthen the black identity. Whites were told they could no longer exorcise their guilt by doing good deeds in the black community; they would be of more help if they combated the racist attitudes and actions of the white community.

The need for identity gave rise to the caucuses in the churches. Some minority groups in the church had been meeting for a number of years, but now they became organized. The first such group was interdenominational and was known as the National Committee of Black Clergymen. They were one of the sponsors of a conference in

Detroit in 1968 that issued the Black Manifesto. This document called on the churches to pay fifteen million dollars in reparations to the black community for the damage done to them by the white community through slavery and discrimination. The money was to be paid into a Black Economic Development Corporation.

The preamble to the Black Manifesto was Marxist in language, and many whites had trouble getting into the document itself. The National Committee of Black Clergymen urged the churches to take the document seriously, and it was this endorsement that made many of us try to respond. Although it was not likely that the churches would pay reparations, they did try to meet some of the needs described.

The Black Manifesto caught the leaders of the churches off guard. We had been going along with our civil rights activities, seeing ourselves as friends of the minorities, quite unprepared to be confronted. It was evident that the white community and the black community were talking past each other.

During this time the Blacks among the leaders of our denomination emerged with new stature. We were dependent on them for guidance on how to move, but they did not let us "use" them in such a way that their credibility in their own community was destroyed. At the same time, we were not prepared to accept all their suggestions without challenge.

John Smith was Moderator of the General Assembly during that year, and he persuaded the General Assembly to invite James Forman, leader of the Black Economic Development Corporation, to address the General Assembly at San Antonio in 1969. John felt the church should hear what James Forman was saying, and the invitation would avoid any attempt to invade the meeting. The day before Forman was to speak, a group of his followers occupied the Presbyterian offices in "475." The staff in charge sent our own staff home, though a few stayed in the offices to be sure someone was present with the occupying group. It was a wise move to send the staff home. Some were refugees from Eastern Europe and violently anti-Communist; others were clearly racist. There would have been some incidents if they had stayed. The groups that occupied the building were quite disciplined and made sure there was no damage to the property.

We were in a revolutionary situation. One of the first casualties of a revolution is trust. People are never quite sure where other people stand on the issues at stake. A second casualty is communication. Things happen so fast that no one is able to keep up or to keep others informed. Everyone is at the mercy of rumors. These factors were to play an important part in what happened in the next few weeks.

The General Assembly in 1969 was indeed a difficult one. Many of the commissioners were unhappy with the invitation to James Forman and equally unhappy that the police had not been called to eject those who occupied the building. The Assembly was verbally assaulted on several occasions. A local political leader of the Hispanic community castigated the Anglos for the suffering they caused his people. The Commission presented a woman from the Caribbean and a youth from South America who blamed us for the problems of that part of the world. The youth's speech was highly inflammatory and drew boos from the audience. Those of us in the agencies were trying to get the church to hear a message about their complicity in some of the problems of the day, but it was a message that most of the church was not prepared to hear. Some of the church was listening, and the breakdown in trust and communication was evident across the church, dividing many congregations. The gap was not just between the agencies and the pew, it was a part of many communities.

We were learning what happens to those who try to stand with the oppressed. John Smith started his year as Moderator with a great store of goodwill and confidence. At the San Antonio General Assembly, when he was the retiring Moderator and George Sweazey was in the chair, the commissioners rejected the leadership of the General Council, of which John was now the chairperson, rejected its proposals, and appointed their own committee to prepare a statement about what the church was facing.

The General Assembly took two actions concerning minorities and the economic situation. It voted that the Board of National Missions and COEMAR should each make fifty thousand dollars available for black economic development. There was misunderstanding in the agency staffs about whether this money should go to the Black Economic Development Corporation or not. The final decision was that it should not go to the corporation but should be spent in other ways. The other decision was to appoint a committee to study ways in which the denomination could become involved in programs of self-development. The events surrounding the Black Manifesto had persuaded people that the present style of church programming was not adequate. This committee was expected to report to the next General Assembly.

By the time we returned to New York the occupying group had left the United Presbyterian floors and had moved to other agencies in the building. This floating occupation was to continue for six weeks, and people never knew when they left their office at night whether they would be able to return in the morning or not. The style of the occupation changed. The occupiers had been very careful of property in our offices, but in other agencies they then began to use office supplies and duplicating equipment to prepare leaflets. They tried to organize the minority workers and called on them to strike. Some of the workers were torn between loyalty to their community and loyalty to the organizations for which they worked. This sort of disruption helped destroy trust. Staff members who had worked side by side for years were uncertain about how to talk to each other, and where two or more were gathered together, there was suspicion.

The staff leaders were unprepared for the situation they faced, and therefore their colleagues were uncertain. No one doubted the integrity and motives of the General Secretaries, but no one was quite sure of their competence in this situation. There was no one with experience in labor negotiations and strikes, yet we were being threatened with them. There was not a minority person in the leadership. Eventually the federal marshals were called in to remove James Forman, and the rest of the occupying group left. There will be many opinions about the value of the occupation—to those who took over the building and to those who attempted to respond. Many of us were sensitized to the issues, we experienced the effects of revolutionary turmoil, we realized how unprepared we were to meet such situations, and we made some agreements to respond to the proposals of minority people.

We still had the possibility of a program for the self-development of people under study. The idea that the people who benefit from a program should have a voice in determining the nature of the program was new to society and to the church. Many institutions had been helping people for decades, but on the institutions' terms. The distinction was being drawn between doing a good deed *for* someone and doing some helpful work *with* someone. In the latter case the idea was to find the way in which people could help themselves. And finding the way for them to help themselves often meant political action to free them from social and economic oppression.

One aspect of this approach that people found difficult to accept was that such programs should not be administered through the normal program channels of the church. The church congregations and the judicatories were a part of community life and therefore a part of the establishment. We were part of the problem, and this fact was true of mission programs and of the church in other countries. If we were to relate to minority people and to poor people, then we would have to move outside the church structures.

The World Council of Churches had been struggling with these same issues. It had sponsored a Consultation on Racism in England just a few weeks after our San Antonio Assembly and had experienced disruption and confrontation. The Central Committee had then taken two hundred thousand dollars from its reserves and started the Program to Combat Racism, the beginning of what was to become its most controversial program. Early in 1970 the World Council held a Consultation on Economic Development in Montreux, Switzerland, and John Smith was one of the representatives from the United States. He described his experience as almost a conversion, for it was in the tension of this meeting that he recognized the need for some sort of new economic order and for a change in the way the churches went about their work. Many staff people from the World Council had difficulty hearing that even their divisions that were involved in helping people, DICARWS and DWME, could not be the instruments for this program. The Commission of the Churches on Participation in Development was to help the churches and church councils change process and shift attitude.

The General Assembly at Chicago in 1970 was one of turmoil. It had to be moved to the Hilton Hotel because other facilities that had been promised were not available. The church had been expressing its concern about American involvement in Vietnam, and some of us had participated in international conferences about relief and reconstruction when there were moments that seemed to promise an end to the conflict, but 1970 was a time when the tensions were reaching a high point. A number of special interest groups wanted to appear before the Assembly, and a special committee was appointed to meet with them and to decide which ones would be given the floor. Several of the alienated youth of that time were present.

This Assembly was also the first one to have Youth Advisory delegates from each presbytery. They had the right to the floor, participated in committees, and made a very positive contribution. One of them suggested a change in the method of electing the Moderator, proposing that the nomination speeches be limited and that the candidates answer questions from the floor. Bill Laws was elected and throughout the Assembly tried to be sensitive to the many different viewpoints being expressed.

The committee to study the self-development of people proposed a program to be funded through adding it to the One Great Hour of Sharing. This approach would help educate the church about the issue; it would not produce much money in the near future. It would also mean a delay of at least a year before the program could begin. It seemed that the minorities were being given the runaround. At San Antonio they had been put off until a new program could be designed; now they were being put off until it could be funded. The "now generation" was not to be put off. There were negotiations in the General Council and discussions in the halls. There was talk of just taking the reserves of the agencies and starting the program, then using the offering to repay the agencies. The Presbyterian Economic Development Corporation had been started by a similar action.

The tension at the Assembly helped many of us realize that the committee's proposal would fall short of what was needed. We also realized that taking a sizable portion of our reserves would wreck our existing work. We hoped that the church not only would start a program for the self-development of people but would go about it in a way that would force the church to change its normal way of operating. One proposal was that each congregation and judicatory and agency reduce its present operation by 5 percent and send the savings to get the program under way. That step would force the reexamination of their work as well as produce money. After much struggle, the General Council reported that it found no solution but to propose the offering approach. An amendment was made that would have taken money from the agency reserves. John Smith sensed that the defeat of this motion would be seen as a defeat of the minorities and that something else had to be done. On the platform he was conversing with the General Secretary of the Board of National Missions, Ken Neigh. When the vote was taken and the amendment defeated, John asked for the floor and said that he and Ken Neigh would attempt to get a million and a quarter dollars from their agencies to begin the fund. There was silence for a moment, and then a standing ovation. There was a sense in which John saved the General Assembly. Bill Laws was so emotional he could hardly speak. It was a euphoric moment for many who were deeply involved in the issue.

My euphoria was dispelled when I walked off the platform. The anger among General Council members could scarcely be measured. Both John and Ken had sat in the General Council meetings and had made no such proposal. They had heard the Council try to protect the reserves of the agencies and had then upstaged them. General Council members could not believe that John had only come up with his idea in the tension of the discussions on the floor.

The members of the Board of National Missions and of COEMAR were not easily persuaded that this move was the right one, and it required some debate before the funds were appropriated. (The Commission served notice on its General Secretary-elect that he should not try similar moves.)

The Committee on the Self Development of People clearly understood that it was not to work through normal church channels. It had people on it who were from the community of need, and these people had plenty of reason to distrust the structures. Similar committees were organized in the presbyteries, and there were times when the presbyteries were frustrated by their inability to veto certain projects. There were times when COEMAR was also frustrated. The committee members assumed they had the competence to judge all requests, even those from other countries. They were not interested in the information we could have shared with them, and they made some mistakes because they lacked such information. They sometimes neglected to talk to our related churches when making a grant in another country. They did give strong support to the wcc Commission of the Churches on Participation in Development. As the program continued, communication between the committee and COEMAR improved, but the committee rightly reserved final decisions to itself.

The social turmoil that brought a new focus to mission also caused a shift in our ecumenical relations. This change was first noted in the national missions activities. The issues of the 1960s gripped us emotionally and affected policies and programs. We were under attack as officials and as persons. Being a part of the power structure and being white meant that we were doubly a part of the problem for the oppressed, and we were trying to correct a century of sins. There was a tendency to move quickly into those actions which seemed possible immediately. There was talk of working ecumenically, but the established organizations seemed slow to respond. People who could work together easily formed coalitions and ad hoc groups. The Interreligious Foundation for Community Organization (IFCO), the Joint Strategy and Action Committee (JSAC), and other coalitions were formed to deal with specific tasks. People felt the need to identify with those who had been ignored by society, and the old bases of unity on theological agreement or ecclesiastical affinity seemed irrelevant. Unity in action for justice was the major concern.

The ecumenical family can no longer be held together by creedal agreement or structural compatability. Each such move to unity is now examined in the light of the place it gives to those formerly excluded from the decision-making process. We are committed to expressions of unity that represent the inclusive and pluralistic nature of the church.

In the late 1960s I participated in a discussion group of mission leaders where James Cone, author of *Black Theology and Black Power*, spoke. His theme was that only Blacks could write theology in the United States. Jesus had come to oppose the oppressors, to set at liberty the captives. Whites are so much a part of the oppressive society that they cannot discern what the liberator, Jesus Christ, has to say. It was an unsettling experience to sit in such a meeting and have yourself dismissed as having no contribution to make to the thought of the church to which you have given your life! The emotional reaction during the discussion period was strong. We were not exchanging ideas but battling about commitment. James Cone had defined himself and the black community in terms of pressure—they were over against the white community. Our task as whites was to make the white community change, to relieve the pressure, and to give him a new opportunity for self-definition. In our efforts to work at this task and to implement our new focus for mission we were drawn into closer cooperation with the other agencies.

10

Adjusting Structure and Style

As the new focus for mission emerged, the Commission on Ecumenical Mission and Relations adjusted its organization and its style of work. A number of forces influenced these changes. The concept of one mission that could not be defined in geographical terms had been one reason for the formation of the Commission. The original mandate to involve the whole church in mission and relations was still a factor in COEMAR's thinking. In addition, the emphasis in the secular world on planning and organizational development influenced many church institutions, and changes in staff personnel provided occasions to rethink structure.

The Commission drew on staff members of National Missions and Christian Education to help study the denomination's ecumenical stance. We called on the Christian Education staff for resources when related churches and regional councils were developing church school curricula. The Association of Presbyterian University Pastors developed international projects through our Student World Relations office. The Board of National Missions carried the United Presbyterian corporate membership in the World Association of Christian Communication. The Council on Theological Education invited overseas students and fraternal workers to their meetings.

The Commission was involved with the other agencies in the development of our church's program on race. The Board of Christian Education prepared to launch a study on racial issues, but in 1963 at the General Assembly in Des Moines, Iowa, it became clear that more was needed. Because the way in which our church dealt with the race problems in the United States would affect our credibility in other parts of the world, COEMAR helped establish the

Council on Religion and Race, in which all the agencies were represented.

The Council on Religion and Race was lodged with the Board of Christian Education for a year and then was shifted to the Board of National Missions, where it had more program responsibilities. The name was also changed to the Council on Church and Race. The Commission was asked to assign a part-time liaison staff person.

The first major program activity in which we became involved was the voter registration drive in Hattiesburg, Mississippi. John Smith represented the United Presbyterian General Secretaries at the opening of the campaign and gave good leadership. The demonstrations and the picketing of the courthouse continued for several weeks, and many of us in the staff took turns participating. We made it a staff project and contributed to each others' expenses, thus avoiding any criticism that we had misused our expense accounts or misdirected mission funds. Many people from colleges and churches went to Hattiesburg to help, and most of them lacked such financial help or the job security we had. We knew we would not lose our jobs for going, but other people were not so sure.

The experience provided insights into the depth of racism in our society and its demonic power in the church. We attended prayer services in both black and white churches. The former were ignoring the demonstrations, with some exceptions, fearing the long-term impact of lost jobs and increased pressures on the black community. The white churches were ignoring the demonstrations, attributing them to outside agitators who had no business in the community. It was Holy Week when I was there, and the Good Friday services in the white churches were conducted as though nothing unusual was taking place in town. Since we had identified with the black community, we felt safe in their ghetto, quite insecure in the white ghetto. The white community was imprisoned in prejudices. They were not free to invite any of us to preach in their pulpits, the black churches were; the whites could not openly discuss all aspects of the issues, the Blacks could. Some progress was made in registering voters, but the general attitudes in the community did not change much during those weeks.

In 1968 the church realized that the nation was facing what has been described as a "long hot summer" of racial tension. There had been riots in Newark, Detroit, Watts, and other communities the summer before. The Board of National Missions was part of an interdenominational emphasis called Crisis in the Nation. A proposal was made by a missionary that the Board of National Missions work with COEMAR to bring back to the United States some fraternal workers to help in the judicatories that summer. The first suggestion was for two hundred to three hundred people. After a study of possible people available and of the assignments, the number was set at seventy-five. We were asking for church leaders as well as fraternal workers, and the invitation to related overseas churches suggested several possibilities, including assigning students from their church who were studying in this country. Some churches released fraternal worker personnel and sent a pastor with them. We finally had sixty-seven persons involved. Assignments were developed, special orientation programs were designed, and it was a good experience. Judicatory staff people came to appreciate the quality of our missionary fraternal worker group, and they also learned of the contribution that churches from other countries can make to our work.

The Commission appropriated $100,000 to pay for the program, and we were challenged on the floor of the General Assembly for using in this country money given for overseas mission. Our reply was that this program, Project Response, was a part of one mission, that the way in which we as a church dealt with the race problem affected what we did elsewhere, and it was an important testimony to related churches that they could have a part in what our church did in the United States.

We referred earlier to the fact that the Board of National Missions was responsible for United Presbyterian mission work in Cuba. The Castro revolution brought difficulty to that presbytery and many pressures into the Synod of New Jersey.[1] Refugees from Cuba migrated to New Jersey, joined some of the congregations, and were critical of the Christians who stayed in Cuba and supported the revolution. When the tensions between the nations became too strong, the church in Cuba decided that it needed to be free from the United Presbyterian Church U.S.A. Because of internal dynamics in the synod there were problems in getting agreement, but they were finally worked out. Since the church in Cuba was now autonomous, the new relationship was transferred to COEMAR. John Smith attended the independence ceremonies. The Board of National Missions staff accepted the logic of the new arrangement and supported the shift. They had been related to these people for years, and it must have been difficult to break the ties. Later another problem arose. When relations between the United States and Cuba were broken and it became illegal to transfer money to Cuba, the Board of Pensions refused to send pensions to pastors who had been in our church's pension plan. The problem was worked out with the help of the World Council of Churches.

The Board of National Missions and COEMAR were both involved in the Caribbean area, and we began some joint programs. The flow of people from that area into the United States resulted in new demands on the national missions programs along the eastern seaboard. The Caribbean Christian Council had member churches that were related to COEMAR and some that were related to the Board of National Missions. The two agencies made a joint appointment of a consultant on Caribbean affairs. He lived in Miami and worked with the judicatories in our church and visited the churches in the Caribbean area to develop the most useful programs in which United Presbyterians could participate.

The immigration of people from South America was affecting more than the eastern seaboard. The growing number of Hispanic people in our nation was shaping our national mission activities and bringing a new factor into our church relationships with all of Latin America. We worked with the synods that border Mexico to develop joint border projects with the Presbyterian Church of Mexico. The concerns were becoming greater than any one agency could meet. We appointed a Consulting Committee on Inter-American Affairs (COCINAC) which was composed of representatives of the General Assembly agencies and certain synods. They held a number of study conferences on Latin America and gave special attention to North American influence in that region. They decided to prepare a United Presbyterian position paper, which would be adopted by the General Assembly. All agencies would participate in its preparation, but the paper would reach the Assembly through Church and Society channels. That approach was good for COEMAR, for it was likely to have controversial parts and we could discuss it with the churches in Latin America more easily if it was not our paper.

The document was called "Illusion and Reality in Inter-American Affairs."[2] Most North Americans thought that we, as a nation, were being good neighbors to the people of Latin America but that in reality we were exploiting them in many ways. The paper claimed that our government, business interests, universities (funded by government and business grants), and to a certain extent the churches, were supportive of a political and social structure that made it safe for us to be there, kept power and wealth in the hands of a few people, and kept most of the people in poverty. Since we could profit economically as a nation from that situation, we used our money and military power to prevent the Latin Americans from making any changes. The first four sections of the paper reviewed the situation and called for restraint by government, business, military, and other interests so that the Latin Americans could be in control of their own lives. The fifth section of the paper talked about church involvement.

The paper was useful in raising issues and showing where the United Presbyterian Church was in dealing with Latin America. We did have the paper discussed in some consultations with churches in Latin America. Some of the schools directed their activities to the poor, and some Protestant leaders saw what was causing tensions within their own circles.

In the follow-up process we were caught once again by our ecumenical failures. The Presbyterian Church U.S. had been invited to attend meetings of COCINAC, but their representatives were not full participants. Yet, when we went to Brazil or Mexico with the statement, they were as much involved with the Presbyterian churches as we were. The staff members of their Board of World Missions were courteous enough to discuss the paper with us, but they had no interest in pushing for a full discussion of it in the two countries where they were involved.

This concept of a global dimension to all of our work is not easy to grasp, and in some cases the implications caught us by surprise. We have already described the situation in Egypt that grew out of the Six-Day War in 1967. However, the effect of that war in the United States was an attempt by the Jewish community to get unqualified support for Israel. I was startled to get a call from a Board of National Missions staff member asking how we could get the United Presbyterians to take a stand along that line. He pointed out that they had been pressuring the Jewish community to support urban programs for Blacks and Hispanics, and the Jews were now coming back with pressure for support of their goals. He was startled to discover we had strong feelings on the Arab side of the question. The war was over quickly and we did not have to deal with the immediate support question. One of the synod executives had accepted an invitation to participate in a mass rally prayer service for the safety of Israel, and managed to be excused when the sudden end of fighting turned the rally into a victory celebration.

One effort to work with the Board of National Missions made no progress. During the 1960s a number of Evangelicals from Egypt migrated to the States. We were concerned that they be helped to find church homes in our congregations, and the church in Egypt was willing to work with us on the problem. When we held a conversation with staff members of the Board of National Missions, they could not see that the situation needed any more attention than any other immigrant group. No special attention was given the problem, and an opportunity to strengthen the churches was lost.

The Middle East became a source of tension with the department of Church and Society, but we were able to resolve the problem. An early statement on the Middle East situation was prepared for General Assembly by the committee of Church and Society. Some parts of it were almost pro-Israel, and many of the fraternal workers serving in the Middle East were quite upset. It was evident that they had been given no opportunity to provide information, nor had the committee that prepared the statement consulted with any of the church people in Arab countries. The idea that this sort of consultation would be appropriate was still new to United Presbyterians. Several of the fraternal workers led opposition to the statement at the General Assembly, and the result was a decision to undertake a more comprehensive study of the Middle East situation. One of the fraternal workers serving in the Middle East was a member of the task force, and the churches in the area were consulted about the problems.

The Commission was responsible for coordinating conversations between our denomination and the Jewish community. Such conversations usually involved the Stated Clerk and representatives of the General Council and the other General Assembly agencies. These conversations had been quite cordial, but they became somewhat strained during the Middle East conflict. The Jewish community had expected stronger support for Israel from our churches. In one of the meetings one of our speakers implied that we could not join them because it would endanger our mission programs in Arab countries. We corrected the statement by pointing out that through such contacts with the churches in the Middle East we received another viewpoint on the situation. We could not support their position because we were not convinced that the Israeli viewpoint was the only one. At the same time we did not fully embrace the Arab position and appreciated our contact with the Jewish community in order to hear their side.

When the United States became involved in Vietnam in the early 1960s, some of the denominations indicated their opposition. We supported statements sent to the General Assembly by Church and Society, but it was not until the mid-1960s that COEMAR became fully involved. Church leaders in Asia protested what our nation was doing. They claimed we were expressing our fear of China, that we were fighting in Vietnam because we counted Asian lives cheap. As American commitment of personnel and equipment increased, so did church involvement. American efforts to get troops from the Philippines, Korea, Taiwan, and Australia involved COEMAR's relations with churches in those countries. The destruction in Vietnam and Cambodia, the bases in Thailand and Laos created problems that involved the churches in relief programs. We found ourselves involved through our responsibility for direct relations with some of the churches in those countries, for relations with ecumenical organizations, for relief programs, and for a ministry to service personnel when they were not on their base. We were also opposed to our nation's involvement in that conflict.

We worked closely with Church and Society and the Council on Church and Race in helping to shape the United Presbyterian position on the war. We worked at supporting relief efforts through the East Asia Christian Conference, the World Council of Churches, and Church World Service.

In addition to these activities where we were in cooperation with the other agencies of the church, COEMAR and the Board of National Missions established some joint offices.

George Todd was Secretary for Urban Industrial Mission in the Board of National Missions. In the late 1950s he had served three years in urban industrial work in Taiwan. George became a staff member for both agencies, and the Joint Office on Urban Mission became the most successful of our combined efforts. Some of the lessons we were learning in the States were shared with other churches, and some of the resources available in related churches were brought to work here. We became an important part of ecumenical ventures through the wcc Division of World Mission and Evangelism.

The Board of National Missions and COEMAR also tried a joint office on medical mission. This effort was not successful. The two agencies had moved in different directions in their medical work. The Commission was still directly involved in medical mission through churches and institutions in other countries; the Board of National Missions had been spinning off its medical work to community-related boards and corporations, organizations that were eligible for government funding. Presbyterian Medical Services of the Southwest managed several clinics and small hospitals that had been mission institutions. The Presbyterian Health Education and Welfare Association was a membership group of workers in church-related institutions and programs, none of which were controlled at the national level. The Board of Christian Education was working on a new program of health and human values, exploring ethical concerns raised by the new advances in medicine. All of these efforts were proceeding along different lines, and the staff people involved could not see much connection.

The plan for a joint leadership development office ran into similar problems of different emphases. The Commission was working with related churches to help them design and implement a plan for leadership development in their own situation. The National Missions staff was processing individual applications and making monthly payments on scholarship programs for minority youth. The programs did not fit together.

In 1965 Margaret Shannon left COEMAR to become Director of Church Women United. She had shaped the ecumenical relations part of COEMAR's work and had developed some new approaches for the church. Ray Kearns, chairperson of the Commission, was called to be the Associate General Secretary for Ecumenical Relations. The structure with two divisions had outlived its usefulness. Mission and Relations had drawn closer to each other, and it was difficult to assign a program to one division or the other. The involvement programs of the Division of Ecumenical Relations looked very much like mission activities, and mission programs had been shifted into the context of church relations.

At the staff conference that year John Smith proposed a new structure that the staff members of the Division of Ecumenical Relations rejected. They claimed that the description of the structure seemed to ignore much of what they had accomplished. There was no time to redesign a structure at the conference, so we reached an interim agreement. We had been through a management study that charted each staff member's accountabilities and showed how the assignments were interrelated. On this basis we could carry on our work. The General Secretary and his associates were authorized to set up interim groupings as needed. We would see what staff constellations emerged as we proceeded, and then we would see if these groupings gave the lead to a new structure. At that conference we failed to agree on a structure, but we reaffirmed our faith in each other as colleagues who could work together. The staff were able to work in that structural limbo for about six months, and in that time we devised a more permanent arrangement.

One of the new management emphases in the 1960s was the formal planning process. Each of the church agencies had someone working at this process at one time or another, and the General Council had a Long Range Planning Committee to coordinate such work. Fred Wilson was transferred from Mass Media Overseas to become our first staff planning officer. He had given excellent service in the mass media, had helped develop the ecumenical work in his field, and had gained the respect of his staff colleagues. Several training courses in planning showed Fred the directions in which he wanted to move, and he became one of the best planners in the church.

A planning process brings changes in the way people go about their work, and it is therefore threatening and tension creating. It changes the way decisions are made and the way money is appropriated. Installing such a process requires the firm support of the General Secretary and associates. In one of our division meetings the staff, impatient with what appeared to be unnecessary extra work, proposed scrapping the whole process. I was in the chair and replied that such a step was not an option. Several Commission members had pressed us to install the process and were anxious to see results. Without such support from the general administration the planning process would have been abandoned. As it was, Fred had some tough sledding, even though he was liked and respected by a very good staff. Later, one of our lay Commission members complimented our staff, saying that we had made the process work with less turmoil than any of the other organizations he knew that had tried it.

During this same period the church was exploring the use of data processing and computers. An interagency committee was trying to develop a unified approach for the denomination, but all that was accomplished was the recognition that the Philadelphia group was going to purchase a Honeywell computer and the New York group was going to rent equipment from IBM. It was assumed that the New York agencies would be doing some of their work in association with other organizations in "475." These actions were before the possibility of telephone line connections to computer terminals.

Installing the planning process and data processing at the same time created its own form of tension. The planning process depended on having information in some new forms that the data processing could supply. However, there was an assumption that data processing was installed to meet accounting needs and that the Treasurer had first call on equipment and operators. When we needed data processing for planning and budgeting, we were often delayed until the department felt it had spare time. We finally had to appoint a committee (proper Presbyterian solution!) to negotiate priorities for data processing.

The Commission's planning was in the system known as Management by Objectives. The first step in such a process is the preparation of a statement of the purpose of the organization. The original statement in establishing the Commission had been an assignment of duties that were already in the life of the church. We had used a statement that had been a part of the foreign mission tradition, but it was not comprehensive enough. A statement of purpose was going to have such importance in the life of the Commission that John Smith proposed a joint staff–Commission member committee. George Sweazey, a prominent pastor and evangelist, chaired the committee. The members worked over a period of two years, getting suggestions, seeking responses to proposals, and so forth. The Commission on Ecumenical Mission and Relations had no purpose apart from the purpose of the United Presbyterian Church, and the latter has no purpose apart from the purpose of the whole church of Jesus Christ. What help would it be to our process if we stated a purpose that could be claimed by every church in the world? We finally decided to quote statements from the Confession of 1967 and from the Constitution which give the United Presbyterian Church's understanding of its purpose, and we then stated our assignment within that framework. It was a fine statement and still has validity. It was approved by the General Assembly, and we referred to it often in our interpretation. (See Preface.)

The next step in our planning was the stating of objectives, and we listed twenty-four of them which covered all of our activities. They not only encompassed what we were doing, they provided direction for future activity. These objectives fell into about ten categories, and we then selected some of the categories for priority emphasis. Staff and Commission members were then appointed to priority groups to plan ways of implementing the priorities. This description of the process shows how the planning process begins to reshape the structure of an organization.

We assigned some new money to implement these priority emphases. It was our hope that the injection of new money would help get the new approaches established so that they could continue when the overall budget had to be adjusted. It is very difficult to reduce a known program for something that is still in the planning stage, but if a new program is under way, it should have an equal chance with an older activity. On the whole, this strategy did not work. We were in a time of ad hoc structures and experiments with new activities. Many of the things to which the priority groups allocated funds were short-term projects or one-shot grants. There were few long-term programs that required sustained funding and set new directions.

It was the assignment of the new money through these priority groups that changed the structure. The priority groups became new power centers for developing programs. Our management consultant had pointed out that the authority to allocate budget and assign personnel was the important power in any organization. Whoever held that power was the real authority in the organization. We had a saying during budget negotiations: "Where two or three are gathered together, you'd better be there too!" The priority groups became the important program units of the organization.

In 1969 Margaret Flory was given the special assignment of exploring new dimensions for mission. She did not explore the established activities such as education, medicine, and evangelism; we had people working in those areas and expected them to be creative and forward-looking. We wanted to find out whether there were other dimensions to our task that needed attention. It was not an easy assignment, for almost any new idea will have some connection to present activity and will seem a threat to someone.

One new dimension was expressed in the program of Bi-National Servants. A number of people within our church had served or studied in another country, still had contacts there, and were committed to establishing a better understanding between the people of the two nations. However, they felt their work would be strengthened if they could work within the life of the churches, and if they could join with other people who had the same idea. It has been a valuable program and has enabled the church to channel the efforts of a number of people who hold a global perspective on their work and who have a deep concern for peace. The Bi-National Servants have expanded their program to include people of other nations who share the goals of the program.

Margaret also explored ways to internationalize mission. The task force that worked with her on the theme felt that this internationalized mission must be directed toward a goal and proposed that the major issue to be addressed was international justice. The new developments in travel and communication had made possible a bringing together of the resources of many different churches and cultures in pursuing such justice. The idea of internationalization of mission has endured, but the focus on international justice has not.

Under the impetus of the participatory democracy patterns that emerged in the 1960s COEMAR invited two missionary/fraternal workers who were on a year's furlough to become advisory members of the Commission.

Their presence at the Commission meeting was quite helpful. Each representative made a report which we sent to all missionary/fraternal workers. The experience was so valuable that it has been continued in the present agencies.

The Commission had been trying to be open to the many voices that were speaking in the church and invited thirty youth to attend one of its meetings. They came from various parts of the church, were between the ages of sixteen and thirty, included minority representatives, and expressed many different viewpoints.

The meeting was one of the wildest that COEMAR had experienced. Some of the radical youth in the group took over the first evening meeting and castigated us for all the sins of the world and the church. There was little dialogue. The Commission members who attempted to reply were dismissed as defensive or were resented because they came back at the speakers in the same terms. By noon the next day some of the moderate voices among the youth assumed leadership, and the group brought in some positive proposals and led us in some celebrations. There were no efforts to repeat such a meeting, but two of the youth representatives were elected as members of COEMAR within a year.

About this time we began holding our Commission meetings at Stony Point to save money. This step turned out to have an even better effect. The setting away from hotels and city distractions, the joint staff–Commission committee work, and informal social events in the evenings brought a new spirit into the Commission's life. We had never had deep tensions between the staff and the Commission, but there were always some. The tension level dropped amazingly in the new meeting atmosphere.

One of the frustrations felt by the Commission members was the result of the thorough work the staff did on the budget. By the time we carried our recommendations to the Commission meeting, it appeared that they could do nothing more than approve. Though we showed how we were implementing their past policy decisions, there was little they could do to change our proposals. We finally worked out a system where we indicated the decisions that needed to be made, outlined more than one option for solving the problem, and made our recommendation among the options. This process was expanded to other aspects of the Commission's work and contributed to a more satisfactory experience for Commission members.

The Commission had been formed during the 1950s when the denominations were in an expanding budget situation. For a year or two we had "end of the year balances" to appropriate. If the congregations gave more money than had been anticipated, or if we spent less than budgeted in some items, we appropriated that extra money as we closed the books. We had to show the denomination that we were spending all the money they gave us. No money from regular mission giving went into reserves.

One of the first budget problems after merger in 1958 was in putting the former United Presbyterian Church of North America missionaries on a salary equal to that received by the personnel of the former Presbyterian Church U.S.A. The United Presbyterian Foreign Board had not adopted the policy of tying missionary salaries to the median of those paid the pastors, and their salaries were at a lower level. The Commission could not have two salary scales, so it was only natural that the lower would be raised to meet the formula. We had been aware of this problem before union, but we had not done the studies necessary to know the size of the problem. The merger came in a year when the average of pastors' salaries went up, so the combination required a sizable allocation to missionary/ fraternal worker support.

Another problem came in providing a budget for the Division of Ecumenical Relations. There had been no program in this activity. The money that had been used was for holding meetings and attending ecumenical gatherings. This money was added to COEMAR's budget, but it still had to be used for the original purposes. Money to pay staff salaries as the division developed and to carry out programs had to be secured through adjustments within COEMAR's resources. There was some tension as traditional programs had to be held level or cut back in order to let the new programs develop.

In the early 1960s we also got into the Untouched Tribes Project in Ethiopia. The Mission in Ethiopia had presented a good plan for expanding into new areas, but there was no new money to provide for it. The increases in giving in the church were tapering off, and increased costs were absorbing all the new money. When the General Mission Budget was being presented to the General Assembly, the Missionary Advisory Delegate from Ethiopia asked where this new program was included. The reply that it was not possible to include it caused a stir among the commissioners. A motion was later presented from the floor that made this project acceptable for extra giving, over and above the regular budget. The motion was approved with enthusiasm.

The plan had identified a number of tribes close to the Mission's area that had never been reached by any Mission or government programs. The people lived in primitive conditions, and the tribes were contained in definite locations. The emperor encouraged the Mission to start such a program. The plan was to establish simple mission posts (in contrast to the elaborate mission stations of a past era), to start a school, a clinic, and a worship center. In one tribe the converts were to be directed to the Orthodox parish which was not far away, but in the other places an Evangelical congregation would be founded. The Evangelical Church was asked to assign evangelists to the project. Five such tribes were reached under this program.

As the Untouched Tribes Project was getting under way, the South Sudan was closed to mission activity. The work in the Upper Nile Mission, as it was called, was a joint program with the Reformed Church in America. Three of their couples from the Sudan were relocated in Ethiopia, and two of them were assigned to the Untouched Tribes Project program. As a trade-off, COEMAR assigned some people to work with the Arabian Mission of the Reformed Church in America.

As early as 1960 we began to make small grants from the reserve funds for the support of the annual budget. Reserve funds were the undesignated legacies that COEMAR received, and we had authority to spend the entire legacy whenever we wished. It was policy to accumulate these legacies as a reserve against emergencies or to ease any reductions that a sudden drop in giving might cause. We turned to this source increasingly as giving did decrease and costs increased. Since the use of reserves was seen as depending on nonrecurring income, we tried to use them responsibly.

As we entered the 1960s we were in need of funds for buildings. Many institutions needed to replace or renovate old structures; others were expanding and needed new facilities. Churches were appealing for funds to lend to congregations that were just getting started. The same need for capital funds was being faced by church institutions in the United States. The General Council began to study a special capital funds drive.

The General Assembly launched a successful capital funds campaign known as the Fifty Million Fund. Church loan funds were established, schools and hospitals were improved and expanded, and the buildings necessary for reaching out to new areas were constructed. Through the Fifty Million Fund we were able to do some things ecumenically that would have been closed to us. The Theological Education Fund needed support for its second phase, and the Christian Literature Fund was just getting started. We also helped the Ecumenical Church Loan Fund of the World Council expand into new countries.

The Commission had an additional windfall of over three million dollars in War Claims—payments made by the United States government to business and charitable organizations that had property in Asia damaged during World War II through American military action. A retired missionary had been working with our property records, and through his good work we were able to document our case. Since most of the damage had been repaired many years earlier through our denomination's postwar Restoration Fund, the Commission was free to use this money for several other mission activities. This War Claims money was used to fund our new priority emphases. It was out of these funds that we were able to help the World Council provide travel funds for representatives of less affluent churches and change the makeup of its major committees. We were able to underwrite Project Response during the Crisis in the Nation program, and we helped to fund the initial costs for some of the racial/ethnic caucuses.

However, the 1960s was a time when the social turmoil undermined confidence in all national structures, whether they were government, business, or ecclesiastical. Financial support was diminishing. In many of the responses that we made to social issues we were convinced we were following the gospel and doing what the church should expect of its agencies. While we knew that not everyone agreed with us, we also knew there were many people who did support our efforts. At times we felt torn between following our Christian commitment and adjusting programs to gain support.

The problem was not confined to giving or to the support of national structures. The social turmoil was affecting attitudes people had about the church, and conflict appeared in many congregations. Membership declined in all the mainline denominations. The Presbyterian Lay Committee appeared as an opposition group, and for a period its efforts seemed to be directed toward undermining the denominational leadership.

Special efforts were made to justify to the church membership the actions of the agencies. An interagency group published a book entitled *Why Is the Church in the World?* [3] Extra resources were put into interpretation, but because we were interpreting actions that were unpopular with a large segment of the membership, we were often working in a hostile atmosphere.

The decade began with some concern about the "decrease of the increase" in the giving to the General Mission Budget, and it closed with some alarm over the "increase of the decrease" in the same giving. The people responsible for interpretation and for raising those funds in the church were working hard. We were regularly assured that the problem was about over, that the slide in membership numbers and in giving had "bottomed out," and therefore we could budget with some optimism. The projections were not accurate and we were balancing our budget with larger appropriations from the reserve funds.

The most difficult pressure in COEMAR's budget was in staff and missionary/fraternal workers' salaries. They were linked to two factors over which we had no control—the median of pastors' salaries and a worldwide cost of living index. Although the total number of people was being reduced as we cut down on new appointments, costs were rising faster than retirements and resignations could compensate.

On two occasions John Smith asked permission to tell COEMAR's problem to the church, but the General Council, which controlled such communications, took the position that the other agencies were facing the same problem. The appeal was from all the agencies, was in general terms, and requested support for the General Mission Budget. The General Council's position was reasonable in a unified budget system; it was also ineffective.

We also sought to increase giving through designated extra giving. The pastors who pressed us for this program were not malcontents but loyal friends who wanted to increase giving in their congregations. We won the battle, and Ada Black gave excellent service in negotiating specific projects for congregations.

The Synod of the Nile heard of our stewardship problems

and offered to send two of its leaders to help interpret the importance of our church's mission program. It was a fine gesture of ecumenical assistance, and we accepted. However, the interpretation staff saw their coming as a burden, not an opportunity. The arrangements were poorly made and the time of these two Egyptian leaders was wasted. We apologized to them for our failure to appreciate their gesture and to use their contribution.

During the mid-1960s the United Presbyterian Church reduced the age of compulsory retirement for staff from seventy to sixty-five. There was pressure in society for earlier retirement in order to open doors for younger people. How strange that such a theory lasted less than fifteen years! John Smith consulted with staff members who had been planning to continue until seventy and worked out an acceptable date. He set his own retirement at sixty-seven and announced it eighteen months before the date. A committee was appointed to seek his successor.

The restructure of General Assembly agencies was under consideration, and there was some discussion about delaying the choice of John's successor. However, the restructure proposal was still being shaped, and COEMAR felt it would be in a stronger position to face the implications of a reorganization if it had a General Secretary, so the search continued.

When the time came, the committee proposed my name. The election was held during that exciting meeting when the youth were present, and for a time I was not sure we would even get to that part of the agenda! John Smith and John Corbin had thoughtfully arranged to have my wife and some members of my family present when the results were announced. There had been attempts to keep the name of the nominee confidential, but my car pool met me on the day of election with a red carpet and a recording of "Hail to the Chief." It was a day to remember.

John Smith still had several months to serve as General Secretary, and I wanted to get acquainted with some of the related church situations. Also, there were several events in which I should participate. Therefore I was out of the country part of the summer and most of the fall. The Commission sent my wife with me on these trips, and it was a great experience to make the visits together. On one occasion, when I became ill, she had to take my place as the honored guest at a celebration. Family situations had prevented our taking advantage of the Commission's plan for the spouse to travel overseas with a staff member on occasion, but we were grateful when it did happen.

A consultation with the Presbyterian Church of Brazil involved representatives of the church, our Mission, and the Commission. Charles Forman, who was ending his term as chairperson of the Commission, was also a part of our delegation. The occasion was a dispute over the transfer of a school to the church, but the discussion covered several issues. The tension between our churches had been developing for a number of years. At the time of a military takeover of the government, the church had established a conservative anti-ecumenical stance and had purged the leadership of its institutions and judicatories.[4] Seminary professors had been dismissed, presbyteries had been dissolved, and several of our fraternal workers had been removed. The Brazilian church claimed close adherence to the Westminster Confession of Faith and expressed concern at our adopting the Confession of 1967. We were concerned about the human rights violations being reported in Brazil; they resented our even raising the question about the integrity of a government that had rescued them from a leftist threat.

The consultation accomplished very little. We were conversing in an atmosphere of suspicion. We resisted transferring the school, even though this step was a reversal of our policy. The Mission had deep concerns that if turned over to the church, the school would be changed. Its service to the community would be destroyed.

The Commission was involved on both sides of the tensions in the Latin America church scene. As a result of our mission history we were related to a number of Presbyterian churches. Though many of them reflected a middle-class mind-set, they had been persecuted minorities and had a tradition of survival. They seemed to feel threatened by the social upheaval about them. Though they did not share all our concerns for the oppressed, they were churches with which we wanted to maintain good relations. However, through our work in student circles and through our ecumenical contacts we were in touch with a number of Christians who were concerned to bring basic social and political change to that part of the world. These people considered the evangelical churches reactionary and irrelevant, and they worked out their understanding of the gospel through coalitions and cooperative mission projects. We provided some support to such projects, even though we did not share their opinion of the churches they had left. Neither group was satisfied with our strategy.

The situation in Mexico was an illustration of differences in approach. The Presbyterians in Latin America defined themselves as people with a conservative theological stand who were not Roman Catholic. In several countries the Catholic Church had used the power of the state to persecute them. Protestants had paid a price for faith. They had fought to survive, and the road to survival is paved with caution. They were anti-ecumenical and suspicious of other groups.

The United Presbyterian Church, on the other hand, was quite ecumenical and open to new relations with the Roman Catholics in the period following the Second Vatican Council. This openness caused great concern to the Presbyterian Church in Mexico. Fraternal workers who participated in public meetings with Catholics were an embarrassment. If we were going to work with that Presbyterian church, we had to respect their autonomy and fraternal workers had to accept their limits. We pointed out that they were asking our fraternal workers to be less than United Presbyterians, but we agreed that the church in Mexico had the right to make such demands. We offered the fraternal workers transfers to other countries if they could not live with the rules.

Further tensions arose with our involvement through ecumenical channels in the student movement, social action projects, and a cooperative theological community. As the centennial of the church in Mexico approached, they asked for a five-year moratorium on all personnel and funds. They wanted to be on their own for a while. We and the Presbyterian Church U.S. agreed. It is the only one of our related churches that voluntarily tried the moratorium approach.

The Nairobi Assembly of the World Alliance of Reformed Churches was the occasion of the merger of the group holding the presbyterian system with the World Conference of Congregational Churches. It was a fine event and grappled with some of the pressing issues of that day. It took a strong stand against the American involvement in Vietnam, and it took an action that amounted to a reprimand of the Dutch Reformed Church in South Africa.

The representatives of COEMAR had gone with the intention of electing the first president to come from one of the third world member churches. I served on the nominating committee, and we were disappointed to discover that the two persons who could have carried the responsibility of president, one from West Africa and one from Taiwan, were unable to attend. Efforts to secure other nominees from third world churches were unsuccessful, and attention was directed toward North America. Bill Thompson had made quite an impression on the Assembly when he presented the new constitution, and he was elected as the first president of the new organization.

A number of member churches were from southern Africa, and the feelings in the Assembly were against the Dutch Reformed Church and its failure to challenge the apartheid policies of the South Africa government. The United Presbyterians had supported the actions which had been almost a reprimand of that church. Our Task Force on Southern Africa had also taken stands in the United States which had caused some concern in the Dutch Reformed Church. The Commission was a part of the task force, but it also had the responsibility for church relations. The representatives of the Dutch Reformed Church asked for a time to discuss a possible visit to South Africa where we could see the situation for ourselves and could talk to some of the people. At the end of the conversation, after we had tentatively agreed to work out such a visit, their representatives hesitantly raised the point that the law might not permit Blacks and whites in our delegation to stay in the same hotels and homes. Our group indicated that it was up to me to reply, so I told them we would not come if we could not stay together. There was no immediate follow-up of this conversation, and the visit did not take place during COEMAR's time.

We went to Addis Ababa for a consultation to discuss a closer working relation between the Mission and the Bethel Evangelical Church of Ethiopia. The church was one of the new members of the Alliance and had been received at the Nairobi meeting. The consultation cleared up some misunderstandings and made some proposals, but not much real progress was made. In spite of many efforts we were not able to establish the communication and confidence that would make for good relations.

The remainder of our trip was in Asia, beginning in Iran and ending in Korea. The only places new to me were Laos and Vietnam. The trip to Saigon was almost aborted because of visa difficulties, and only after thirty-six hours of combined farce and tragedy did we work our way through the problems and get to see our son, who had arrived a week earlier as a medic in the army. It is a strange world where the army maintains a public relations officer whose assignment is to make arrangements for traveling parents to contact their soldier children!

We saw at first hand the destructive power of a large military operation. It not only damages the land with military action, it disrupts the society and the economy with its presence. The large influx of personnel, money, and materials is a spur to immorality and corruption of every sort. Vientiane in Laos, Bangkok in Thailand, and Saigon in Vietnam were the cities we saw which had felt the impact. Though the churches worked hard at relief operations and social programs, they could not offset the great damage.

The trip through East Asia was an affirmation of all that COEMAR had worked for in the transfer of power to the churches. In my first trip to the "mission fields" in 1954 I was received at airports by delegations, met in villages with celebrations, and generally treated as a power figure. I was the new secretary of the Board of Foreign Missions. Sixteen years later I was the new secretary of an organization with a much larger budget and less power. The world and the churches had changed. The world had become more urbanized, the cities more sophisticated, and the churches more self-sufficient. Several of the churches did not know what to do with me. Church leaders were busy and had little time to spend with someone who had little impact on their work. We had hoped for just such a development, and I came home feeling that we had accomplished much. I was treated much as church leaders from other countries get treated when they hit the rat race of New York. I was being treated as an equal.

One illustration of this change to modern life occurred in Korea. My first visit to that country was in 1958 when Seoul was still recovering from the war. The streets were filled with potholes, and vacant lots were filled with refugee shacks. I preached at the famous Yung Nak congregation which had three services each Sunday morning. However, the approach was casual and informal, people wandering into the services at any time. In 1970 I was invited to preach again, and we then had lunch with the pastor, Dr. Kyong-jik Han and some of his associates. In their conversation they discussed the elder who had prayed so long in one of the early services that the service went overtime. In twelve years they had become more sophisticated. Seoul was now a modern city with freeways and traffic problems, and the church has adapted to the urban culture.

One of the first matters I had to take up was the selection of an Associate General Secretary. Black Presbyterians United, our United Presbyterian caucus, had agreed to work with me in selecting a minority candidate. They presented the name of Oscar McCloud, and I was happy that he agreed to come. He had been on the field staff of the Board of Christian Education and on the staff of the Council on Church and Race in the Board of National Missions, and COEMAR would profit from his having had those experiences.

In 1971 the General Assembly approved a reorganization that would merge COEMAR into a new structure at the end of the following year. We had just eighteen more months as an organization. That action set the main emphasis of my work as a General Secretary—to prepare for an orderly transfer of COEMAR's work. We also had come to the point where the budget had to have some radical reductions. The proposals for reordering our priorities were also ready for action.

The staff had proposed that our priority objectives be four: Communicating the Gospel, Equipping Christian Communities, Participation in God's Redemptive Action in the World, and Expressions of Unity for Churches and Mankind. (We were still using sexist language!) We organized the staff and the Commission around these priorities, examining all of our work in the light of them.

We determined to enter the reorganization with a strong program and a policy framework that would carry the new organization through a couple of years of uncertainty, what we termed a shakedown cruise. We went ahead with priority determination, budget reduction, adjustments in salary patterns, and so on, in an attempt to get as many things in shape as possible.

The budget reduction was our most difficult problem. I had chaired the staff budget committee for a number of years, so I could not escape responsibility for the problem. Two years before, I had warned that we were counting too much on reserves, but we were still getting assurances from the General Council that giving was going to go up. The giving continued to drop, and we had reached a critical point.

My proposal was to reduce the missionary/fraternal worker staff by two hundred people over a period of two years, and the COEMAR staff in equal proportion. That meant cutting four executives and their support staff. I assumed the responsibility for making the recommendation, but the staff supported me.

The Commission recognized that we were dealing with people's careers and their sense of missionary calling. It was only after much discussion and with considerable reluctance that they took the action. We said we would work in every possible way to help people stay in their assignments, but that we could not assume responsibility for them in the Commission's budget. We tried to use our priority determination process to help us in making the cuts, but it was difficult to deal with personnel in those terms, especially when related churches were involved.

We immediately started discussions with churches and institutions abroad. We asked them to say who the people were that they most wanted to keep, and we then asked what they could do to help some of them stay in service. We discovered that several institutions were prepared to supply all or part of the personnel support of people working for them. We had a category of Overseas Associate for people who worked outside the United States on another organization's support but whose activities contributed to the mission of the church. A number of these people then took this status to keep their ties with the church.

We also agreed that where a congregation in this country wanted to raise extra money and send it to support specific personnel, we would work with them on the arrangements. This step was a promotion of special designations, and there was protest from some quarters. We replied that the careers at stake were more important than the rules.

The most vigorous discussion was with the General Council of the Synod of Pennsylvania. The members claimed we had never warned them of the situation. I reminded them of the letters John Smith had signed with the other General Secretaries, but it was clear that only a drastic action such as we had taken could get their attention. They offered to help us with the problem. The Commission welcomed this initiative. We agreed to supply a list of persons who needed to be supported at least until the time of their next furlough. The amount required over the next two or three years was over $400,000. I attended the meeting in which the program was presented to the presbytery executives, and they agreed to take on the challenge. Other congregations across the church tried to help us, and during the final year of COEMAR's existence our special designated gifts were over a million and a half dollars.

This task put much extra work on some of our staff. Ada Black spent long hours working out the designations from congregations. The Regional Secretaries visited the related churches abroad and discussed their decisions about personnel, and they then had to counsel with the persons involved. A missionary on furlough from Iran was assigned to help people who needed relocation. The Ministerial Relations Office in Columbus assigned one staff person to help the ordained personnel find churches. The initial action we took assumed that some people would have to be brought back from overseas before their term was complete, but with help from the Synod of Pennsylvania and other sources all were able to finish their terms.

The reduction in New York staff was also difficult, and we struggled long with the problems. The Administrative Council worked with me to determine what posts we considered necessary, but the decisions about the reductions were mine. We tried to keep as many people available for the new structures as possible, but we still had to abolish three positions.

A proposal from the Mission in Ethiopia presented us with another situation that required special attention. The follow-through on our consultation in Addis Ababa had not been very successful. The Mission was still an operating organization and felt that many of the opportunities before it were not being addressed. The Mission proposed to send two representatives to meet with the Commission and express their concerns. The staff expressed anxiety that one country might get undue attention from the Commission, but we also recognized that neither the staff nor the Executive Committee could shield the Commission members from such an approach. It was important that the Mission have the chance to have its say. So we appointed a special committee to meet with the representatives and examine the Mission's requests. Africa was to be Oscar McCloud's concern as an Associate General Secretary, so he met with them.

The Mission had not sought an action from the Evangelical Church on their proposals, so the committee recommended that Oscar visit Ethiopia and join in discussions with the church. There were some positive responses to the presentation, but the Commission kept the matter in balance with the rest of its responsibilities.

The Mission representatives expressed both surprise and appreciation for the way in which they had been received and their proposals considered. Although they had not gained approval on all they had sought, they had been heard.

During these months we also faced a difficult situation with the missionary/fraternal workers in the Middle East. These included a number of people who were not assigned to work within the churches but rather in institutions that were related to, though not controlled by, the churches. The churches accepted agreements about providing for the needs of the fraternal workers, but the proposals were not always implemented.

Many of the people we appointed to the Middle East were uncertain about where they fit into the total structure. In some cases they thought of themselves as representatives of the United Presbyterian Church, while COEMAR had sent them to be a part of the church or institution in that country. We urged them to find their place in the context of that church, to make their way with the people with whom they were working; they thought they should be conversant with everything the United Presbyterian Church was doing in the area and be in on decisions about the use of all resources we sent there. Their frustration with this difference in viewpoint came out in a move to assert what they considered their rights. The fraternal worker group in Egypt, Lebanon, and Iran sent representatives to meetings where they prepared a plan for a regional organization of United Presbyterians serving in the Middle East. This organization would control all United Presbyterian resources spent in that area.

The Commission agreed to have representatives go to the Middle East to meet with them and to discuss the proposal. I felt quite sure the churches, which had not been con·

sulted about such a plan, would have none of it; it was a denial of all we had worked for in church-to-church relations.

We discovered that the fraternal workers in Egypt were not enthusiastic about the proposal, though they wished we had ways of keeping them informed and of seeking their insights. They felt they had a good relation with the church. Among the fraternal workers in Lebanon and Iran there were different opinions, and those who did work closely with the church did not want that relationship disturbed. They emphasized the importance of our keeping them informed about our programs, and they expressed their desire for a chance to share their opinions and insights with us. There were still some who hoped that the plan would be implemented, and we held a meeting with the church leaders to discuss it. They would have none of it. We stressed again the importance of arranging for the fraternal workers to relate to the churches, and how important it was for the churches to do their part in making the people we sent effective in their work and helping them feel at home.

These problems came at an important time. One of the policy papers we were working on for adoption during these last few months was called "The Role and Style of the United Presbyterian Church in Mission and Relations Through the Commission on Ecumenical Mission and Relations."[5] We stated our efforts to have as broad a forum of discussion as possible, but we would not desert our commitment to working with other churches.

11

Preparation
for Reorganization

The restructure of the United Presbyterian Church was the result of discussions and developments that had been under way for years. There had been proposals for reducing the number of synods in order to fit the demographic patterns of the nation. For example, three synods were involved in the New York City metropolitan area, and two synods divided the metropolitan area of Philadelphia. The desire to develop church strategy for the massive urban complexes of our nation was strong in the 1960s. The possibility of regional synods was one pressure toward restructure.

The Board of National Missions had distributed the control of mission programs to the synods and presbyteries in which they were located. The national missions budget process involved the synods, and synod representatives sat on many of the Board committees. The presbytery was considered an instrument of mission, and many of the social action programs of the 1960s were conducted by presbytery committees. This pattern of distributing responsibility for mission programs to the middle judicatories was one development that led to restructure.

There was also a feeling among some people that the denomination should have one mission program and that such a unified approach would never come about as long as the three major agencies were autonomous and in control of their own finances. The way in which John Smith and Ken Neigh upstaged the General Council at the Chicago General Assembly was a favorite illustration (see chapter 9). The desire for stronger control over agencies of the General Assembly was also a factor in the reorganization.

There was also a heavy populist spirit in the land, and people were developing a distrust of all large organizations. To them the General Assembly agencies seemed to go their own way, funding activities such as a community organization in Rochester against the Kodak company or grants through the World Council to liberation movements in Africa. One accusation against the agencies was that they would take action in a presbytery whether the presbytery wanted them to or not. Most of the illustrations were exceptions to the agencies' normal patterns, but critics usually latch on to exceptions to make their point.

Several movements were converging—regional synods, power of the agencies to be shared with the synods and presbyteries, and centralized control of General Assembly agencies. A group convened by the General Council had been discussing some revisions of the General Assembly structure for some months, but it did not make much progress. They did propose that a new committee be authorized by the General Assembly. A major reorganization was under way.

The Committee on Reorganization did considerable consulting. There were representatives of the agencies in their membership. In one COEMAR meeting the committee presented a draft proposal which was quickly rejected. Perhaps none of us wanted such a major overhaul of the system as was under way, and no proposal would have satisfied us. On another occasion the Executive Committee was asked if there should be an overseas mission unit as an identifiable part of the new structure. The staff members in the meeting argued against this approach, for it seemed to turn back the clock to the foreign mission concept. We felt that geography was not an adequate basis for the delineation of mission responsibility, and our close working relationships with the Board of National Missions would be endangered. In this point we differed from the Presbyterian Church U.S., which was also in a restructure program and was including a Division of International Mission.

The plan was released in plenty of time for study before the General Assembly. At the General Assembly a special standing committee would be appointed to examine the plan and make recommendations to the plenary. The Commission's Executive Committee took the position that we would be considered vested interests and therefore it would be inappropriate for us to propose amendments. We therefore proposed six questions that we wanted the special standing committee to consider as they examined the plan. We thought they might be able to make some changes in answer to the questions. This strategy was the wrong approach. If we had prepared specific proposals on the changes we thought should be made, the special standing committee would have given them a fair hearing. There were commissioners who were unhappy with some aspects of the plan, but they needed specific proposals to support. The Commission was not opposed to the entire plan, but some of the uncertainties about the power and responsibilities of the agencies could have been clarified.

The Board of National Missions and the Board of Christian Education had taken similar approaches to the Assembly. The presentation of the plan to the Assembly had spoken about all the vested interests that would be affected by the reorganization, and all of us found it very difficult to participate. The plan was approved with a few minor changes.

The next step was to appoint a Committee of Eleven to work out the details of the proposal. Sherman Skinner chaired this committee, and he was committed to working with the agencies in developing the details of the structure that would take over their work. Staff members were given many opportunities to make proposals. Much time was given to preparing descriptions of work and assembling information that would help the committee and the new agencies.

A staff team was appointed from Christian Education, National Missions, and COEMAR to propose a structure for the Program Agency. Oscar McCloud, who had served on the staff of each of the agencies, was the chairperson. The mood of the time was for much participation in decisions, for plenty of opportunity for the different voices in the church to be heard. They prepared a structure that recognized this theory but would have been far too expensive to implement and almost impossible to manage. I make that statement from the clarity of hindsight, but I defended the plan before the Committee of Eleven.

The Committee of Eleven reported to the General Assembly, the membership of the new agencies was elected, and the process of transfer was started. The new agencies had six months to get organized, become acquainted with their new responsibilities, and prepare to assume responsibility on January 1, 1973. The General Secretaries of the existing agencies were invited to meet with the new Program Agency in order to answer questions. On one occasion they were asked to present the work of their agencies. A group of our staff helped me prepare an audiovisual presentation of five case studies that illustrated the type of work we were doing and the problems we were passing on to the new agencies. George Bushnell, the first chairperson of the Program Agency, always treated us with courtesy and called on us for comments on many items before the group.

' In COEMAR we tried to establish confidence in the new agencies. Some of our elected members would be serving in the new boards to provide continuity. We tried in various ways to help some of the new members come to know us and to be known. Members from the three agencies—Program, Vocation, and Support—were invited to participate in the study conference with missionaries and fraternal workers. The new General Directors were invited to address COEMAR's final meeting. We were encouraged that two of them, Don Smith and Oscar McCloud, had been called from COEMAR's staff.

Any transfer of responsibility is accompanied by a great amount of anxiety. I had helped bring about such transfers in the careers of missionaries and some Commission Representatives. Suddenly it was happening to me and to my staff colleagues. We were insecure about the future, not only about our careers but about the work into which we had poured so much of our lives.

One of the lessons I had learned in the church union of 1958 is that truth and valuable ideas endure on their own merits. One does not have to negotiate for their preservation. What is necessary is that activities be examined with open minds.

The basic approach of merging mission and unity has endured because it was right. Over a period of fourteen years the Commission on Ecumenical Mission and Relations opened new possibilities in the life of the churches, blazed new paths in mission and relations, and made a lasting impact on the lives of many people.

Notes

Preface

1. *Minutes of the Commission on Ecumenical Mission and Relations of The United Presbyterian Church in the U.S.A.*, November 1967.

2. W. Stanley Rycroft, *The Ecumenical Witness of The United Presbyterian Church in the U.S.A.* (Philadelphia: Board of Christian Education, The United Presbyterian Church in the U.S.A., 1968).

3. The supporting scripture references most often referred to are Matt. 28:18–20 (the Great Commission); Acts 1:6–8; Rom. 10:14–17. One of the most thorough scriptural studies is in *The Missionary Nature of the Church*, by Johannes Blauw (New York: McGraw-Hill Book Co., 1962).

Chapter 1: Prelude

1. Quoted by R. Pierce Beaver in *Ecumenical Beginnings in Protestant World Mission* (New York: Thomas Nelson & Sons, 1962), pp. 20–23.

2. *All Things New*, Preparatory booklet for the Fourth Assembly of the World Council of Churches (Geneva: World Council of Churches, 1968), p. 19.

3. A fuller description of the National Council of Churches structure of 1950 is given in *Christian Faith in Action* (New York: National Council of the Churches of Christ in the U.S.A., 1951), pp. 263–273.

Chapter 2: Preparation

1. *Minutes of the General Assembly of The United Presbyterian Church in the U.S.A.*, 1957, Journal, p. 256.

Chapter 3: In the Beginning

1. The denominational youth staff was a team composed of the Youth Secretaries from each of the General Assembly agencies.

2. Comity agreements were developed in order to cover all areas of the world with mission activity. They also helped avoid competition and duplication of work. For example, comity agreements meant that the United Presbyterians worked in Egypt and the Presbyterians in Syria and Lebanon. See Beaver, *Ecumenical Beginnings in Protestant World Mission,* pp. 15ff.

3. The former Boards of Foreign Missions had felt the need to have staff closer to the mission fields in a time of rapid change. The field representative posts were created in the early 1950s and were considered a part of the board staff, not the mission staff.

Chapter 4: Leadership and the Developing Organization

1. *An Advisory Study* (New York: Commission on Ecumenical Mission and Relations, The United Presbyterian Church in the U.S.A., 1961), p. 3.

2. John A. Mackay, *Ecumenics: The Science of the Church Universal* (Englewood Cliffs, N.J.: Prentice-Hall, 1964), p. 14.

Chapter 5: Early Emphases

1. Bishop Samuel was a leader in the Coptic Church council that assumed responsibility for directing the church's affairs when Pope Shenuda went into seclusion during a dispute with President Sadat. In this responsibility Bishop Samuel was on the official platform during a military parade and was one of those killed during the assassination of President Sadat.

2. *Minutes of the General Assembly of The United Presbyterian Church in the U.S.A.,* 1963, Journal.

3. John Rosengrant, ed., *Assignment Overseas* (New York: World Horizons, 1960).

4. Partners in Obedience was the theme of the International Missionary Council meeting in Whitby, Ontario, in 1947.

Chapter 6: An Advisory Study

1. *An Advisory Study* (New York: Commission on Ecumenical Mission and Relations, The United Presbyterian Church in the U.S.A., 1961).

2. The Commission Representative for the Caribbean–Central America area was stationed in Mexico and covered several countries. Therefore each Mission had a secretary who related directly to the Commission offices in New York.

3. *An Advisory Study,* p. 7.

4. "Partnership in Mission," COEMAR minutes, 1964, Nos. 64–148.

Chapter 7: Changes in the Role and the Support of Missionaries

1. "The Stewardship of Human Resources," COEMAR minutes, June 1966.

2. "The Development and Deployment of Missionary/Fraternal Worker Personnel," COEMAR minutes, November 1967.

3. "Executive Salary," COEMAR minutes, June 1967.

Chapter 9: A New Focus for Mission

1. International civil servants are people employed by organizations such as the United Nations, the International Labor Organization, the World Health Organization, the World Council of Churches, etc. They feel torn in identity between the international milieu in which they work and the nation from which they come.

2. Donald Black, "Focus on the White Liberal" (Board of National Missions, The United Presbyterian Church in the U.S.A., 1967).

Chapter 10: Adjusting Structure and Style

1. The Presbytery of Cuba was a part of the Synod of New Jersey.

2. "Illusion and Reality in Inter-American Affairs," *Minutes of the General Assembly of The United Presbyterian Church in the U.S.A.*, 1969.

3. Lewis S. Mudge, Jr., *Why Is the Church in the World?* (Philadelphia: Board of Christian Education, The United Presbyterian Church in the U.S.A., 1967).

4. A full description of this part of Brazilian church history has been published by Joao Dias de Araujo under the title *Inquisitions Without Burnings*, tr. James N. Wright (Rio de Janeiro: Instituto Superior de Estudos da Religiao, 1982).

5. "The Role and Style of the United Presbyterian Church in Mission and Relations Through the Commission on Ecumenical Mission and Relations" (New York: COEMAR, 1971).

Bibliography

All Things New. Geneva: World Council of Churches, 1968.

An Advisory Study. New York: Commission on Ecumenical Mission and Relations, The United Presbyterian Church in the U.S.A., 1961.

Araujo, Joao Dias de. *Inquisitions Without Burnings*. Translated by James N. Wright. Rio de Janeiro: Instituto Superior de Estudos da Religiao, 1982.

Beaver, R. Pierce. *Ecumenical Beginnings in Protestant World Mission*. New York: Thomas Nelson & Sons, 1962.

Blauw, Johannes. *The Missionary Nature of the Church*. New York: McGraw-Hill Book Co., 1962.

Bridston, Keith R., and Walter D. Wagoner, eds. *Unity in Mid-Career*. New York: Macmillan Co., 1951.

Christian Faith in Action. New York: National Council of the Churches of Christ in the U.S.A., 1951.

Hogg, William Richey. *New Day Dawning*. New York: World Horizons, 1957.

Mackay, John A. *Ecumenics: The Science of the Church Universal*. Englewood Cliffs, N.J.: Prentice-Hall, 1964.

Minutes of the General Assembly of The United Presbyterian Church in the U.S.A., 1958–1972.

Mudge, Lewis S., Jr. *Why Is the Church in the World?* Philadelphia: Board of Christian Education, The United Presbyterian Church in the U.S.A., 1967.

Rycroft, W. Stanley. *The Ecumenical Witness of The United Presbyterian Church in the U.S.A.* Philadelphia: Board of Christian Education, The United Presbyterian Church in the U.S.A., 1968.

Smith, John Coventry. *From Colonialism to World Community: The Church's Pilgrimage*. Philadelphia: Geneva Press, 1982.

van der Bent, Ans J. *Voices of Unity*. Geneva: World Council of Churches, 1981.

Index of Names

73884

DATE DUE

DEMCO 38-297